# Globalizing Pentecostal Missions in Africa

## The Emerging Missionary Movement in the Africa Assemblies of God

Papers from the Pentecostal Missions Consultation
organized by the
Africa Assemblies of God Alliance
World Missions Commission
in cooperation with the
Acts in Africa Initiative

Limuru, Kenya
April 28-29. 2011

Editors
**Denzil R. Miller**
**Enson Lwesya**

**Globalizing Pentecostal Missions in Africa: The Emerging Missionary Movement in the Africa Assemblies of God.** © Acts in Africa Initiative. All rights reserved. No part of this book may be reproduced, stored in a retrieval system, or transmitted in any form or by any means—electronic, mechanical, photocopy, recording, or otherwise—without prior written permission of the copyright owner, except brief quotations used in connection with reviews in magazines or newspapers.

**Individual copyright notices**
"Planting Churches among Unreached Peoples," © Dick Brogden
"Response to Dick Brogden," © Uchechukwu Ama
"Review of Dick Brogden," © Andrew Mkwaila
"Globalizing Pentecost in Africa," © Denzil R. Miller
"Response to Denzil R. Miller," © Lazarus Chakwera
"Missional Mentoring," © Antonio Pedrozo and Brad Walz
"Response to Pedrozo and Walz," © Enson Mbilikile Lwesya
"Missional Tensions," © William Kirsch
"Response to William Kirsch," © Douglas Lowenberg

Library of Congress Cataloging-in-Publication Data
Miller, Denzil R., editor, 1946—
Lwesya, Enson Mbilikile, editor, 1967—
**Globalizing Pentecostal Missions in Africa: The Emerging Missionary Movement in the Africa Assemblies of God** / Denzil R. Miller and Enson Mbilikile Lwesya

1. Missions   2. Pentecostal   3. Africa

ISBN 978-0-9882487-6-2

Printed in the United States of America
    2011 - AIA Publications, Springfield, MO, USA
    2014 - AIA Publications, Springfield, MO, USA

# Contents

Introduction ........................................................................................ 5

Official Communiqué ......................................................................... 7

1. Planting Churches among Unreached Peoples: How Do We Partner in Actively Reaching These UPG's?
   *Dick Brogden* ............................................................................. 11

2. Response to the Paper by Dick Brogden
   *Uchechukwu Ama* ..................................................................... 37

3. Review of the Paper by Dick Brogden
   *Andrew Mkwaila* ...................................................................... 59

4. Globalizing Pentecost in Africa: How Can We Proactively Emphasize Pentecost and Mission in Africa and Beyond?
   *Denzil R. Miller* ....................................................................... 63

5. Response to the Paper by Denzil R. Miller
   *Lazarus Chakwera* ................................................................... 81

6. Missional Mentoring: How National Churches with Strong and Effective Missions Outreaches Can Mentor Those Without?
   *Antonio Pedrozo and Brad Walz* ............................................. 85

7. Response to the Paper by Pedrozo and Walz
   *Enson Mbilikile Lwesya* .......................................................... 111

8. Missional Tensions: Theological Training Systems and Compassionate Ministries in African Missions
   *William Kirsch* ......................................................................... 127

9. Response to the Paper by William Kirsch
   *Douglas Lowenberg* ................................................................ 159

Appendices

> Appendix 1: Resolution Calling for a "Decade of Pentecost" ......... 175
>
> Appendix 2: Vision 5:9 Fast Facts ....................................... 176
>
> Appendix 3: Latin American Statement on Cooperation ............... 178
>
> Appendix 4: Missions Together: An Intensive Training Seminar for Missional Leaders .................................................... 180
>
> Appendix 5: Missionary Categories: A Latin Country, 2010 .......... 182
>
> Appendix 6: Compassion and Justice in the Old Testament ............ 183
>
> Appendix 7: Cover Letter for Resolution Calling for an AAGA World Missions Commission .......................................... 185
>
> Appendix 8: Resolution Calling for the Establishment of the World Missions Commission .......................................... 187
>
> Appendix 9: Constitution of the Africa Assemblies of God Alliance World Missions Commission ............................... 189
>
> Appendix 10: List of Participants: Pentecostal World Missions Consultation ......................................................... 193

Contributors ................................................................. 194

Other Decade of Pentecost Publications ........................................ 197

# Introduction

God calls His Church—including the African Church—to actively participate in His mission to redeem fallen mankind. We have been called to join with Him in urging all people of all nations to appropriate the finished work of Christ on the cross. Thus the missionary mandate, which is clearly evidenced in Scripture, is core to all of the Church's activities in the earth. History, however, has demonstrated that missions work has never been easy, nor is it inexpensive. Admittedly, there are many legitimate reasons why the church in Africa struggles in performing its task of preaching the gospel to all nations. While a course on the challenges of the missionary enterprise in Africa may indeed be welcomed, it is essential that we reflect deeply on the subject. In doing this we must go beyond simply itemizing Africa's weaknesses and glorifying its fears. We must look for practical answers to the challenges we face. It was to that end that this book was compiled.

The papers contained herein were first presented at a historic "Pentecostal Mission Consultation" held on February 28-29, 2011, in Limuru, Kenya. The consultation was held under the auspices of the World Missions Commission (WMC) which is a constituent organization of the Africa Assemblies of God Alliance (AAGA), from which it derives its authority. The WMC has been given the solemn responsibility of facilitating, by whatever means possible, the missionary mandate of the Lord on behalf of AAGA. Therefore, by the very nature of its establishment, the WMC relies heavily on the human, intellectual, and financial resources of its members.

Each presenter and participant at the Consultation is appreciated. I sincerely appreciate the leadership of the AAGA Executive Committee and the great partnership of the Assemblies of God World Missions (US) and its constituent organizations that work together with us in Africa as we strive to truly be the salt and light of the earth. Special mention goes to Dr. Denzil R. Miller, director of the Acts in Africa Initiative with whom we grappled concerning the purposes and premise of this 2011 Pentecostal Mission Consultation. Finally, appreciation goes to the regional representatives of the WMC for their support in this endeavor as together we seek to awaken the missionary zeal of our respective regions and become God's catalysts to rekindle an organized missionary advance that will impact generations to come.

Our chief desire during the Consultation was to hear the voice of the Spirit in regard to His strategies for going about the missionary task. We further sought to answer the question, how can we do this together? During the short time we were together, we sought to open our minds and hearts to allow the Lord of the Harvest to confront our past and incorrect assumptions, while challenging us to rise up together in our collaborative strength to go to preach the gospel to all nations before our Lord's soon coming. We trust that the Lord will use this book as He used the Consultation to facilitate the actualization of the *misso Dei* in Africa and the world.

Enson Mbilikile Lwesya, D.Min.
Chairman
AAGA World Missions Commission

# Official Communiqué
## Pentecostal Missions Consultation
## World Missions Commission
### Africa Assemblies of God Alliance
### Limuru, Kenya

[Note: This Comminiqué was unanimously adopted by the delegates attending the Consultation on April 29, 2911. For a list of participants of the Consultation see Appendix 10.]

We the representatives of the various churches and agencies within the Assemblies of God family in Africa in a Pentecostal Missions Consultation organized by the World Missions Commission of the Africa Assemblies of God Alliance held in Limuru, Kenya, 28-29 April 2011, listened to the reading of and responses to the following scholarly papers:

1. "Unreached People Groups in Africa: How Do We Partner in Actively Reaching these UPG's?" by Rev. Dick Brogden (with a response by Rev. Uche Ama);
2. "Globalizing Pentecost in Africa: How Can We Proactively Emphasize Pentecost and Mission in Africa and Beyond?" by Dr. Denzil R. Miller (with a response by Dr. Lazarus Chakwera);
3. "Missional Mentoring: How Do National Churches with Strong and Effective Missions Outreaches Mentor Those Without?" by Rev. Antonio Pedorzo (with a response by Dr. Enson Lwesya);
4. "Missional Tension: Theological Training Systems and Compassionate Ministries in Missions (Africa)" by Dr. William Kirsch (with a response by Dr. Doug Lowenburg).

After deliberating on the above papers, and the responses to these papers, we made the following affirmations and declarations, resulting in this official Communiqué:

1. That this first Pentecostal Missions Consultation has indeed addressed some of the basic issues relating to the task of evangelizing the African continent in the twenty-first century. These issues are especially pertinent during AAGA's Decade of Pentecost emphasis (2010-2020);

2. That the papers and discussions highlighted certain pressing needs in the missionary advance of our Africa Assemblies of God fellowships during this important Decade, including the following:

   a. The need to strategically focus on evangelization of Africa as rapidly as possible, with a twofold focus on the unreached Islamic peoples of North Africa and the greater Arab World and the remaining unreached peoples of sub-Sahara Africa and the Indian Ocean Basin;
   b. The need to create an information database on these above-mentioned unreached peoples to be shared with our constituent national churches. This project should be viewed as a continuous process;
   c. The need to develop strategic partnerships across the continent between the national churches affiliated with the Africa Assemblies of God Alliance;
   d. The need to develop a strategic prayer network focusing on the unreached peoples of Africa, and to connect this regional effort with the global prayer initiative of the World Assemblies of God Fellowship (WAGF).
   e. The need for missional mentoring among our national churches as a means of strengthening and building capacity within all of the national churches of the Africa Assemblies of God.
   f. The need to develop a truly biblical and missional model for compassion ministries, all the while remaining focused on the core mandate of the church, that is, reaching the lost for Christ.

That in furtherance of the ongoing task of fulfilling the *mission Dei*, the Consultation affirms the following:

1. That the Decade of Pentecost initiative (2010-2010) declared by the Africa Assemblies of God Alliance at its quadrennial General Assembly in Johannesburg, South Africa, in 2009 be enthusiastically embraced by all of our national churches.
2. That, in preparation for the greatest evangelistic and missionary advance in the history of the Africa Assemblies of God, each of our national churches seek to globalize Pentecost and missions in all of their churches and among all of their members in accordance with the goals of the Decade of Pentecost.
3. That the AAGA/MC affirms the global mandate of the Great Commission, and consequently endorses, encourages, and supports initiatives to evangelize the Arab and non-Arabic Muslim World. While we affirm that reaching the Muslim world constitutes the Church's greatest challenge, we also encourage national churches to accelerate their efforts at targeting all of the unreached peoples of Africa.
4. That the Africa Assemblies of God move quickly to develop active regional, national, and local prayer networks in cooperation with the World Assemblies of God Global Prayer Initiative.
5. That the AAGA encourage missional mentoring between national Assemblies of God churches with strong missions programs and national churches with emerging, yet less-effective, missions programs.
6. That the Africa Assemblies of God employ biblically-informed compassion ministry as part of its mandate to reach all peoples with the gospel before the soon coming of Christ (Matt 24:14), and further, that a contextualized biblical theology of compassion ministry be developed to inform and undergird this ministry.

Adopted this 29th day of April 2011

# Planting Churches among Unreached Peoples: How Do We Partner in Actively Reaching These UPG's?

DICK BROGDEN

BACKGROUND

Pentecostals have always prided themselves on being Spirit-led. We sometimes claim to be so, even when circumstances have contributed greatly to the leading. In the 1930's most missionaries from America travelled to their fields of service by sea. During World War II the Germans began to torpedo Allied shipping in the Atlantic, and Japan overran most of the countries of the Pacific Rim. The only safe region to travel to was Latin America; therefore, the majority of American missionaries sent out in the 1930's and 1940's were sent to Central and South America. These missionaries labored through much difficulty and resistance to plant indigenous churches. Itinerating missionaries shared both testimony and challenge in US churches, inviting many to give, pray, and come join them. Many did, and Latin America became the most populated of missionary fields. Was this the Spirit, was it circumstance, or was it a wondrous combination of both?

The role of data in determining missionary call has not always been warmly welcomed by Pentecostals.[1] There are various reasons for this. One reason is understandable: missionary research into unreached peoples has unfortunately sometimes led to managerial missiology and an overly-pragmatic approach to missions. Vinoth Ramachandra warns that because managerial missiology is based on capitalism, the Western church has been shorn of its prophetic voice.[2] In the late 1990's in Khartoum, Sudan, Luis Bush and the AD 2000 Movement stormed into town looking for churches to adopt unreached peoples in Sudan. In a rushed meeting of church leaders, hands were raised to indicate that certain peoples would be adopted, a list was checked off on a computer, the meeting was adjourned, Bush stormed off to another meeting in another country, and nothing whatsoever happened to reach the unreached. Maps, statistics, and seven-year plans have sometimes been used to generate a lot of heat, but not much light nor result. Some Pentecostal leaders look warily at the latest methods and passing fanfare, and point to the explosive growth of the worldwide Pentecostal church as unplanned, orchestrated by God not man, and above data and research.

In 2011, however, unreached people group data has continued to be verified, refined and cross-referenced. Three major research entities, *The World Christian Encyclopedia,* the International Mission Board of the Southern Baptists, and the AD 2000 and Beyond Movement, all collaborate with themselves and others—like SIL and their Ethnologue—to give ever- more accurate data about where and who the unreached are. As Alan Johnson rightly says, "We cannot pretend to not know what we know."[3] Some resistance by Pentecostals to the role of data in determining missionary call and placement is not laudable. Some of it is defensive. Some of our resistance to data is actually resistance to the Holy Spirit. The Holy Spirit in this hour is forcefully bringing to our attention the reality that there are thousands of distinct people groups in the world who have no adequate access to the gospel. Some people groups[4] are unreached (witness-bearers present without the missiological breakthrough[5] that Ralph Winter described) and some are unengaged[6] (no one even working with them, no missionaries, no Bible, no churches, no indigenous Christians).

Pentecostal missions and mission leaders, therefore, sometimes resent the role of data and research as it points out our distribution problem. There is adequate gospel to cover the globe, but our missionaries, our prayers, and our dollars tend to be concentrated where the most Christians are. Muslims, Hindus, and Buddhists comprise half the world, three billion people. Of these three billion, 86% (more than two billion) have no access to a church or even a Christian friend. Meanwhile, 97% of mission money and activity is from Christian people to Christian people.[7] God forgive us for being defensive about deployment. We cannot blame the Spirit for our disproportionate deployment of missionaries. None would explicitly argue that God loves some countries and peoples more than others, yet that exact implicit case is made when we defend our current status by claiming it was Spirit-led. If there is a lack of missionary presence among certain peoples and religious blocks, it is certainly not the intention of a cosmos-loving God, nor is it His fault. God give us the courage to believe that the missionary Holy Spirit can use accurate data to help reveal His will for His missionary people.

The success of the international missionary efforts of the Assemblies of God family has led us to ask the wrong question. We often ask, "What is the church accomplishing around the world, and how can we celebrate it?" In this urgent eleventh hour, the Lord of the Harvest still leaves the ninety-nine who are found to seek the one who is lost. The better question to serve as a framework for all our efforts is, "Where does the church not exist, and what are we going to do about it?" Let us covenant to be a missionary people who are Spirit-led and data-informed.

As the Holy Spirit leads us to understand the times, peoples, and religious blocks of the world and wrestle with what we should do, we quickly realize that "O Lord, the sea of peoples is very big, and our missionary boat is very small." We also realize that our efforts to this point have been nominal at best. The Holy Spirit is the Spirit of Truth and let us not fear to admit that, in the work of reaching unreached peoples, our African Assemblies of God churches have not yet lived up to our Lord's expectations. Our potential and promise is vast, our effectual work is small. More than a decade ago I attended an Eleventh Hour Institute in Lilongwe, Malawi. Since that time, numerous other institutes have been held. There has been impressive rhetoric but little reality. The missionaries we have sent have largely been sent to work with other established churches, or to countries that have sizable Christian populations, or they have not lasted, or they have become discouraged and are ineffectual in the work. We have run into financial and practical obstacles that have limited us. We have encountered relational and spiritual stress that has caused us to stumble. We have been attacked by demonic forces that have sobered us. We stand at a crossroads: we will either falter and fail, or wipe our bloodied nose and press in again to the fight, wiser, braver, wounded, yet stronger for it.

God's great missionary heart does not allow us to think small. God's unlimited Spirit refuses self pity. We stand bloodied but unbowed before the task, holding in tension our limited resources and God's great mandate. How do we settle this tension? We must maintain a heart for the whole world even as we focus on specific peoples.

I propose to this conference, and to the AAGA family, that even as we hold to God's heart for the world, we approach our task by apportioning it into strategic steps that He empowers us to discern and to take. Jesus himself, bearing passion for every tribe and tongue and nation, had a specific call limiting himself to the "lost sheep of Israel."[8] Recognition that we are part of the missionary people of God around the world, and that we do not have to do everything we could do, frees us to adopt a specific focus. While Africa only has minority Hindu and Buddhist peoples, we have over 300-million Muslims on our continent. I recommend to this conference that AAGA and the World Missions Commission prioritize our attention on countries that have little or no indigenous churches and that have majority Muslim populations. I further recommend that we focus first on the unreached Muslims of North Africa. I suggest that we do this as an initial step in our obedience to take the gospel to the whole world. I, therefore, propose that we adopt a strategy that sequentially targets unengaged or unreached Muslim peoples in the following areas:

STAGE 1: Muslim peoples of North Africa and Somalia (Mauritania, Morocco, Algeria, Tunisia, Libya, Egypt,[9] Somalia, and Northern Sudan)

STAGE 2: Muslim peoples of the Arabian Gulf (Saudi Arabia, Yemen, Oman, UAE, Bahrain, and Kuwait)

STAGE 3: Muslim peoples of the Middle East (Palestine, Lebanon, Jordan, Syria, and Iraq)

STAGE 4: Muslim peoples of Central Asia[10] and Turkey (Iran, Afghanistan, Pakistan, Bangladesh, and North India)

STAGE 5: Muslim peoples of Asia (Indonesia, Malaysia, Western China, and Southern Philippines)

STAGE 6: Diaspora Muslim peoples in the West[11] (France, England, and Germany)

When, by God's grace, we have church-planting missionary teams in each of the above countries, we will convene again to broaden our scope. Let us covenant to be a missionary people that bear God's passion for the whole world, even as we allow Him to lead us to a priority and sequence of focus.

Let our first focus be the unengaged Muslim peoples of Mauritania, Morocco, Algeria, Tunisia, Libya, Egypt, Northern Sudan, and Somalia.

PARTNERSHIP

The focus of this paper is, therefore, effective partnership to reach the unreached people groups of East Africa. I have made a case in my introductory remarks that, if we are to be effective, we must recognize the times and ask the Spirit to lead us to a specific and narrow focus for our joint partnership. We will not be effective if our goals are too broad and indistinct. We must have clear, focused, and strategic aims that are agreed on and sacrificially embraced. I have urged upon this fellowship that the focus initially be the unreached Muslim peoples of Mauritania, Morocco, Algeria, Tunisia, Egypt, Northern Sudan, and Somalia. The remainder of the paper shall propose practical means for effective partnership for these peoples. The principles espoused shall be general enough to apply to any effort among unreached peoples in Africa.

**Partnering by Prayer**

Sudan Interior Mission, which began in Nigeria in the colonial era when sub-Saharan Africa was referred to broadly as "Sudan," has a wonderful and simple motto, "By Prayer." If we are to effectively partner to reach unreached peoples in Africa and beyond, it will only be by praying together. This type of prayer must be modeled by our leaders:

> Apostolic leadership is absolutely essential to launch and sustain a church-planting movement. These apostolic foundation layers bring people together for prayer, challenge others with vision, discern how to equip and empower members in the body and then release them for ministry. They are catalytic leaders, and they are not content to pastor a church. They must be about setting new foundations upon which others build the church.[12]

I, therefore, propose that AAGA/WMC establish Friday of every week as a day of prayer and fasting for unreached peoples. Every AAGA-related church will be encouraged to host a noon prayer meeting for unreached peoples. (Many churches do this already in the form of a Jumaa Prayer Fellowship for Muslims, and this can be pursued and developed in cooperation with the Assemblies of God World Missions, Global Initiative ministry,[13] formerly called the Center for Ministry to Muslims.) I further propose that a prayer coordinator be mobilized whose full-time job includes producing a weekly prayer bulletin that is disseminated by post and e-mail, organizing prayer seminars in every AAGA-member country, identifying and empowering a prayer coordinator in every AAGA-member country who continually mobilizes prayer, and leading prayer journeys to targeted countries and peoples.

Let us covenant to be a missionary people who pray together and pray unceasingly for unreached peoples. Let us dedicate Friday as a day of prayer and fasting in all our churches. And let us appoint a prayer coordinator to the AAGA/WMC whose primary role is to travel the region and mobilize prayer for the Muslim peoples of Africa.

**Partnering by Collaboration**

Our Pentecostal identity must be as humble as it is unapologetic. Some missiologists refer to the last one hundred years as the "Pentecostal Century." Some theologians divide Christendom now into three major spheres: Catholic, Protestant/Evangelical, and Pentecostal. Much too large to be contained by our human constructs, the Holy Spirit has surged in first (Classical Pentecostalism), second (Charismatic Renewal) and third waves. And now the church worldwide increasingly accepts and celebrates the Pentecostal movement. One of the unsung contributions of the Pentecostal movement has been our emphasis on proclamation. Pentecostals in their fiscal poverty have had to keep the gospel Christ-centered and Spirit-empowered. Historically we did not have the resources to run huge programs or invest in international social remedies. We focused instead on the gospel core: what God has done in Christ. Ray Bakke says it well,

> The gospel of Jesus Christ is not advice; it's news. A fundamental difference between Ann Landers and Jesus Christ is that Ann offers advice and Jesus offers news. The gospel of Jesus changes everything inside our own prisons, be they personal, family, community or national. The gospel is never advice, and it's never a program. It's news!...the Spirit empowers real and total

change…. We patronize the poor when we give them advice. But Jesus is news, not advice.[14]

Robert Webber agrees,

Social action is an essential aspect of the church's work in the world—peace and justice and caring for the poor, widows, orphans, the disenfranchised, and the marginalized arise from true faith. But these actions are to result from the embodiment of God's full narrative, not from a Christianity accommodating itself to Western culture's doctrine of progress and utopia.[15]

John Stott, the framer of the 1974 Lausanne Covenant, explains that, while both evangelism and sociopolitical involvement are Christian duties, "reconciliation with man is not reconciliation with God, nor is social action evangelism, nor is political liberation salvation."[16]

Pentecostals have always acted socially without losing their passion for souls and a hunger for the justice that can only fully be realized when Jesus returns. Having won the battle for increasing mainstream acceptance, we should neither relent from our emphasis on preaching nor move the goal posts to accommodate a human-centric approach to God's kingdom or His mission. Now more than ever, we must do mission in Pentecostal power. Other mission agencies want to partner with us *because* we are Pentecostal. They come to our schools and seminaries; they invite us to their councils and boards *because* of who we are. This is not the time to be moderate; this is not the time to pull back from the essence of Holy Spirit dependence. Now more than ever, Pentecostal missionaries are needed. We are needed for our clear vision on spiritual realities. We understand the spirit of Islam, and we understand how it must be challenged as evil, even as all evil spirits have been cast out since our Lord and His apostles ministered. This is true in church history as well:

Records show that when seekers (this is what they were called) enrolled in the catechumenate process, the first question asked of them was, "Do you renounce all false worship?" This declaration was made publicly, in front of the assembly, prior to being admitted in the catechism and beginning the process of being conformed to the image of Christ. Because of this declaration (i.e., renouncing all false worship), the rumor spread that Christians were atheists and subversive anarchists bent on overthrowing the Roman government. For this reason they were persecuted.[17]

Now more than ever, Pentecostal missionaries are needed and wanted. We could make one of two mistakes: we could be so glad that we are wanted that we give up our Pentecostal praxis, or we can be so proud of being needed we refuse to partner with the wider body of Christ.

We must not fall into either one of these traps. We must be more Pentecostal than ever (dependent on Holy Spirit power for witness) and we must be more lowly than ever before. The reality is that we need the wider body of Christ as much as they need us. We have much to learn, much to be led into. We cannot afford even a hint of Pentecostal pride. We must acknowledge both what we have to give and what we desperately need to receive. We will only effectively partner together to reach the unreached if we do this as unapologetic Pentecostals who humbly learn from and collaborate with the wider body of Christ.

I, therefore, propose that the AAGA/WMC become a full member of Vision 5:9. Vision 5:9 is a consortium of more than 75 Evangelical mission agencies dedicated to a church-planting movement among every Muslim people group by 2025. The goal is twofold. The first benchmark is to have every Muslim people group larger than 100,000 people engaged by 2012. There are 214 of these groups left in the world. The second benchmark is to have every Muslim people group engaged by 2025. There are more than 2,221 of these.[18] The Vision 5:9 partnership produces materials for prayer, mobilization, and best practice for those working among Muslim peoples, and would be a tremendous blessing to us if we elect to participate. (A fast-facts overview of unengaged Muslim peoples around the world is noted in Appendix 2.)

Note in the table below that almost 80% of all unengaged African Muslim peoples, numbering more than 100,000, reside in Northern Africa. This figure increases when you add Mauritania and Somalia. A second imperative for partnership by collaboration is with the consortiums that have formed for every country in North Africa and the Middle East. These include the Blue Med (Mauritania, Morocco, Algeria, Tunisia, and Libya), the Red Sea (Horn of Africa), and the MEMPC (Middle East Muslim Peoples Consultation), and others.

These consortiums are multi-agency, multi-denominational, and multi-national. Their annual consultations bring together local Muslim-background believers, missionaries, media representatives (satellite, radio, orality, Internet), donors, intercessors, and prospective workers. They are incredible for networking, information, prayer, and relationship building. If AAGA is to

| Macro-Region | Region | Counts and Sums | Less than 100,000 Population | More than 100,000 Population | Total |
|---|---|---|---|---|---|
| Africa | Eastern Africa | Count of Unengaged =>100000 | 58 | 13 | 71 |
| | | Sum of Population | 1,610,705 | 4,299,266 | 5,909,971 |
| | Middle Africa | Count of Unengaged =>100000 | 61 | 5 | 66 |
| | | Sum of Population | 1,059,884 | 687,586 | 1,747,470 |
| | Northern Africa | Count of Unengaged =>100000 | 154 | 59 | 213 |
| | | Sum of Population | 4,241,659 | 38,377,965 | 42,619,624 |
| | Western Africa | Count of Unengaged =>100000 | 112 | 11 | 123 |
| | | Sum of Population | 2,151,036 | 2,567,868 | 4,718,904 |

effectively partner to reach the unreached Muslim peoples of North Africa, we cannot do so unless we participate in these forums. There is much wisdom to be gleaned and many mistakes that can be avoided by learning from others. We need, however, to move beyond participation in these consortiums, towards leadership. In 2001 in Northern Sudan four missionary leaders (one Assemblies of God, two Southern Baptists, and one representative of Open Doors) sat together and began to ask the basic question, "What can we do better together than separate?" This question led to the formation of a ministry network that is dedicated to working together to see a church-planting movement among all Muslim peoples of northern Sudan. The American Assemblies of God missionaries in Sudan have helped lead this network from its inception, and it has grown to include Anglicans, Presbyterians, Catholics, Baptists, Sudanese, Asians, Latin Americans, Africans, and Europeans. Working groups for prayer, media, training, mobilization, women, believers from Muslim backgrounds (BMB's)[19], sport, and children have all emerged. Specific partnerships for Beja, Darfur, Nubians, Nuba Mountains, and northern Sudanese Arabs have been encouraged. Best of all, there is an incredible synergistic spirit of unity and partnership among all who work among Muslims in Sudan. The tenth annual consultation finished in February 2011 with just under 100 representatives from around 35 different agencies and 15 different countries.

A third vital opportunity for collaboration for the AAGA/WMC is with the emerging Assemblies of God fellowships in North Africa. The separation of North Africa from Africa and into the Middle East by the American AGWM is not binding on AAGA. Though these churches are infant and tiny, we should seek relationship with the leaders of the Assemblies of God across North Africa and invite them to full membership with us. We should send representatives from the AAGA executive leadership to meet with the emerging leaders of the Assemblies of God in these North African countries so that we may encourage them and see how we can best collaborate with them in the future.

Let us covenant to be a missionary and Pentecostal people who humbly collaborate with other kingdom-minded workers ministering among unreached peoples. Let us pursue membership in the Vision 5:9 partnership and encourage our missionaries in context to be a vital, contributing, and leading part of every evangelical consortium that seeks to plant churches among unreached peoples. And, let us proactively pursue relationship with the emerging Assemblies of God fellowships in North Africa.

**Partnering in Teams**

If we are to be effective in reaching the unreached people groups that remain in the world, we must do so by participating in multi-national, multi-agency, and multi-generational church planting in teams. Such arrangements have strong biblical precedent[20] and current logistical necessity. Multi-faceted teams are like a many-sided diamond. Different backgrounds afford different gifts and opportunities, and the more varied the team, the more capable they are to respond to the fluid context they are resident in. Indian church planter, Paul Gupta, declares,

> While there may still be a significant place for the well trained, western, cross-cultural church planter, the growing edge of mission today is strategic partnership, coming along side the national church and mission task force, and working together to reach the unreached.... The national church in India does not yet have the economic or human resources to meet this need.... Educated western missionaries, who are willing to serve under national church and mission leaders, can have a profound impact equipping, mentoring, and supporting a national mission force.[21]

Gupta is right when he says that missionaries who chose to serve under national mission leaders can have a profound impact. He is biblically wrong when he infers that local churches cannot resource their own missionaries, and when he suggests a subservient role for either partner.

Multi-faceted teamwork is certainly true of the Assemblies of God community in Sudan. In 2011 the Assemblies of God missionary team is made up of 50 adults. The youngest team member is 21, and the oldest is in his mid-sixties (multi-generational). We have representatives of seven nations, including Germany, South Africa, Paraguay, Malawi, Switzerland, and America (multi-national). We have representatives of the Assemblies of God from four different nations, and also members from the Dutch Reformed Church and a Swiss house church (multi-agency). This diversity has certainly helped us over the years. If we want to buy a piece of property we send the Malawian; if we want to meet a government official, we send the German; and if a demon needs to be cast out, who better than the Paraguayan! Of course, this example is hyperbolic to make the point, but the reality remains that all cultures and backgrounds offer advantages and disadvantages, and a multi-faceted team can better cover weaknesses while empowering strengths.

Such teams are not without their tensions. Differences of culture and language acquisition impact team meetings and interaction. Discrepancies of financial support necessitate honest discussions and creative sharing. Missionaries with less support have to be willing to live at a simpler level than others, and missionaries with more support have to be willing to be generous and open with their resources. Leadership roles and member responsibilities have to be clearly defined, and expectations must be constantly clarified. A memorandum of understanding (MOU) must lay out the structure, theology, and missional praxis of the team, and all who join the team must agree to live by its provisions.

There are many ways to partner together in team, but these ways can be generally grouped into two essential types: secondment and joint ventures. In a secondment model, the established team and team leader is the authoritative partner. Missionaries wishing to join that team must agree to serve under the current leader and what is laid out in the MOU. For our purposes, this means that another missionary could be seconded to an AG team, or we might second our missionary to another team. In a joint venture, two established teams, who both have a leader and an MOU in place, agree to work together. How that cooperation will unfold is worked out between the leaders (alternating leading meetings for example). Each team leader is responsible for his or her team, but the teams agree to collaborate closely for certain meetings (such as prayer and strategy) and independently for others (such as pastoral care and team renewal).

Church planting in teams is a relatively new concept for the Assemblies of God, though other mission agencies have been striving to do so for several decades.[22] In 2010, the East Africa region of US AGWM launched their "Live Dead" initiative, an effort to mobilize, train, and deploy teams of American missionaries to plant churches among the unreached peoples of East Africa. This initiative was birthed out of the conviction that American missionaries in East Africa have neglected to pioneer in the difficult places and among the resistant peoples, and that God has not rescinded His apostolic call on Americans to take the gospel where it has not yet reached.[23] Intrinsic to this vision is a desire to partner with the established national churches of East Africa in reaching these unreached peoples. Two principles converge in this effort: obedience to the call of God on Americans to pioneer among the unreached, and the commitment to do so wherever possible in partnership with the African church. These Live Dead teams are AGWM teams, complete with a MOU and team leader who reports to a team leader overseer, who in turn reports to the AGWM area director, all of whom from the beginning hope and intend to work in joint venture with AAGA-supported missionaries whenever possible.

I propose that we form multi-national teams made up of both AAGA and other AG members from around the world who have an agreed-upon leader (African or otherwise) and MOU, and who are trained and then deployed among the targeted Muslim peoples of North Africa. I propose that AAGA/WMC and AGWM intentionally seek to mobilize, train, and deploy eight multi-faceted teams, made up of Africans, North and South Americans, and other AG members, where possible, by 2015. Let us mobilize at least one team for each of the North African countries of Mauritania, Morocco, Algeria, Tunisia, Libya, Egypt, Northern Sudan, and Somalia.

The process of team formation should include certain basic elements: Each AAGA member country shall identify and commission one mature missionary couple and support this couple fully.[24] AGWM shall identify and commission one veteran couple for each of the appointed North African countries. Other AG partners from around the world shall also be invited to contribute one missionary couple. These couples shall be trained together for entry into their country of service. During the training, leaders shall be appointed and the team shall be formed. The leader may be an African or a non-African. A team MOU shall be drafted by the team leader and submitted to the team for input. After the MOU has been agreed upon, the team shall deploy to their North African location. These teams shall be considered joint-venture AGWM/AAGA teams, and blessing shall be requested in writing from the AGWM Area Director for North Africa and the Middle East (currently Mark Renfroe) for the AGWM missionaries on these teams. If, in some cases, there is not enough personnel to form a complete team, the WMC shall seek out a like-minded team from another agency already on the ground in North Africa and second the missionary couple to that team.

Team bonding is more important than formation, and much harder to achieve. Intensive effort must be spent on understanding one another and accommodating cultural differences within the team. Cultural acceptance can make or break multi-national teams. Patrick, the great apostle to Ireland, understood this well. Concerning Patrick, George Hunter writes,

> The fact that Patrick understood the people and their language, their issues, and their ways, serves as the most strategically significant single insight that was to drive the wider expansion of Celtic Christianity, and stands as perhaps our greatest single learning from this movement. There is no shortcut to un-

derstanding the people. When you understand the people, you will often know what to say and do, and how. When the people know that the Christians understand them, they infer that maybe the High God understands them too.[25]

Let us covenant to be a missionary people who partner together to place a multi-faceted church-planting teams in Mauritania, Morocco, Algeria, Tunisia, Libya, Egypt, Northern Sudan, and Somalia by 2015. Let eight AAGA-member national churches fully support a catalytic missionary couple from their country. Each AAGA missionary couple will join with an AGWM couple to form eight church-planting teams in North Africa. These teams can serve as factories for more church-planting teams, similar to the model of the Celtic monasteries:

> Within the threefold division of the day into worship, study, and work, monastic communities were beehives of wide range of activities. The community worshiped together, perhaps twice daily, they learned much of the scriptures together—by heart, especially the psalms. They nourished each other in a life of "contemplative prayer" and many monastic communities also functioned as "mission stations," preparing people for mission to unreached populations.[26]

The time has come for collaborative and prayerful teams who are able to reproduce themselves and send forth other teams with independent leadership. We must start somewhere, however, so let us commit together to these eight strategic countries and dedicate ourselves to the establishment of eight reproducing teams.

**Partnering in Creative Access**

There are many positive examples of cross-cultural missions endeavors in the AAGA family among near-culture peoples. The church in Burkina Faso has been an excellent example of this by sending missionaries with a small grant into neighboring countries where they work as tentmakers until they plant a church and teach the congregation to support themselves through tithes and offerings.[27] This model, however, will not work for missionaries who are sent to North Africa. Neither will it work for western entities to support African missionaries. Gupta unwittingly provides a negative example when he writes,

> To financially sustain the movement I had sought funding from various partners in America and Europe...those funds and the accountability for them became a source of contention among state leaders. When we could not agree on the structures of accountability, that disagreement seemed to fuel other reasons for pursuing separate paths.[28]

If external support inevitably leads to division and separation, a way must be found to support African missionaries from within Africa.

A hardworking pastor in Malawi survives on less than $300 (US) per month. He does so with the help of a small garden or farm, the convenience of public transport, the help of government schools, the benefits of socialized or subsidized medicine, and the proximity of extended family and Christian community who can help in times of crisis. A home missionary sent to the Yao along the southern lakeshore in Malawi can live under much the same conditions, and a missionary sent from Malawi to Zambia can leave his children with extended family, board a bus, and in less than a day be in his new country with new Christian friends and a similar economic situation. But what about the Malawian who goes to Sudan? He must pay for air tickets, international school prices, and mega-city rents. He has no extended family to help in crisis; he has huge medical costs in sickness that are not subsidized; and he can grow no vegetables in his small city apartment because of both space and heat. Living modestly, as simply as his pastor back home, takes more than $2000 (US) per month.

One reality of mission to the peoples of Muslim North Africa is the financial cost. If African missionaries are going to make it in these contexts, they need at least $2000 per in monthly support. This figure is untenable emotionally to a constituency whose normal wage is a tenth of that amount, and it is untenable financially if we are to send multiple missionaries from each country. We have hit the "gold ceiling." Great passion to do mission in North Africa and beyond has crashed on the unforgiving rocks of financial reality.

This reality has been met and surmounted in Sudan through a creative partnership between AGWM and the Malawi AG. The Mwamvani family of Malawi has survived for a decade in Sudan modestly supported by their sending church and largely supported by their tent-making role made possible through infrastructure laid down by AGWM missionaries. In Sudan, the broader missionary team has legal registration through a local business entity. This entity is registered with the government as an educational business and runs community centers, English centers, and schools. These schools function as non-profit businesses, meaning they charge fees for services rendered but no gain is allowed to stockholders. All profits pay the salaries of the staff or are reinvested to upgrade the business. The Mwamvani family has worked in these educational centers, and, in return, the centers have provided a vehicle and offered a salary of almost $1000 per month each.

The combined salary, matched with the $200 per month they receive from Malawi barely covers food, rent, transport, phone, and medical needs. This is a model that has worked for a decade, can work for a few select more, but is not reproducible on a grand scale. There are, however, principles that can be drawn from this model that can point the way forward for the future.

The first principle is that missionaries sent by AAGA into North Africa must have a marketable trade. If they are doctors, teachers, engineers, developmental workers, or other such professionals, it is increasingly possible for them to be gainfully employed in North African contexts. We must, therefore, commission such missionaries with the same status we give ordained applicants. We cannot make the twin mistakes of counting them as lesser missionaries or giving them less training.

The second principle is that of a "way-maker." Once a missionary from an AAGA-related national church is established, and not living hand-to-mouth or in crisis mode, he can begin to prepare the way for others from his country to join him. This, then, is the rationale for one missionary couple to be supported at $2000 a month with $10,000 in work funds. If sending AAGA-related national churches can support one couple fully—alleviating constant pressure to survive—that couple can then dedicate a significant portion of their time to making a way for others to join them through tentmaking roles. I propose that, in each country where we send a missionary team, we create an employment business. The supported couple's role will be to pioneer a business that specializes in job placement. Working as a liaison between North African businesses, schools, and development agencies, this platform matches job opportunities in North African contexts with waiting missionaries back home.

Some of these opportunities may be simple, labor-intensive roles. Eritrean and Ethiopian women are being employed throughout the Middle East as cleaners and nannies. These jobs are difficult and often these women are abused, but they have access into the strictest Muslim homes as servants of Christ. They pray for sick Muslim children, they share their faith with cloistered Arab wives. The Moravian missionaries were not too proud or too fearful of indentured service—nor should we be. The employment agency could provide cleaners and professors, guards and graduates to the universities of North Africa. A finder's fee of one month's salary (paid by the employer) is the normal service charge, and these fees can, in due time, run the business. Ray Bakke gives some helpful insight into the process of establishing credibility in new contexts:

> You don't start by planting churches. You plant ministry that "scratches where people itch" in the name of Jesus. The ministries will generate the necessary ingredients for healthy churches in the long run: first, indigenous leadership; second, local funds. People who come into urban communities from outside with timetables for church planting almost inevitably create the church in the image of the outside leaders. They usually require long-term sustaining funds as well.[29]

I, therefore, propose the following: Let each country strive mightily to fully support one couple at the above level with the understanding that this level of support is not reproducible, and that its purpose is to give a solid foothold in that country so that others can be brought in as paid tentmakers. These initial businesses will require start-up capital. This is true whether they be an employment agency, an English school, or any other business venture. I propose that the multi-faceted team together take the challenge of raising the start-up capital for these businesses—even if that means the majority of the money comes from the AGWM members of the team.

Let us covenant together to be a missionary people who partner together in establishing businesses that can make a way for tentmaking missionaries to thrive in North Africa. Each AAGA country shall support one capable and mature missionary couple who will serve as way makers for others, and AGWM shall shoulder the responsibility for raising the investment capital that is needed for the success of the venture.

## Partnering in Training

In order to be successful in deploying church-planting teams among the unengaged Muslim peoples of North Africa, we must partner together in training. With the exception of Somalia, each of the proposed targeted countries is Arabic-speaking, and all of the countries have Muslim majorities. Multifaceted teams are, in the long run, the most fruitful and, in the short run, the most contentious. Extended training that is undertaken together is essential if we are going to overcome the stress of cross-cultural cooperation. Current models of Bible school training are not adequate for the work of planting churches among Muslims. Paul Gupta says of Indian seminarians, "The Bible College became the place they came to buy time and determine whether or not they were called to the ministry, a place of extended childhood."[30] We must not denigrate college education, but with Gupta "I have concluded that formal education is ill suited and cannot effectively equip evangelists, church planters, and apostolic leaders for ministry."[31]

I, therefore, propose that AGWM and AAGA cooperate on a North Africa-based, two-year training program for new joint-venture missionaries. Let all sixteen couples (eight supported by their national churches and eight supported through AGWM) be ready for deployment by January of 2013. Let these sixteen couples first be sent to Libya (or another North African location) to study Arabic for two years. In the course of this study they will be trained in Islamics, missions, cross-cultural communication, spiritual warfare, team life, and tentmaking. At the end of the two years (January 2015), these missionaries will be deployed in teams of a minimum of two couples (one AAGA and one AGWM) to the eight targeted countries.

I further propose that AGWM initially provides a missionary couple to run this language school and lead the church-planting training center, establishing it by August 2013 as a viable entity, able to provide student visas. These sixteen couples would comprise a training team that we lead for two years. Upon successful completion of the training program, eight new multifaceted church-planting teams will be launched into North Africa. These sixteen couples should be viewed as a minimum.

Since Muslim ministry in the North African context is so radically different from the Sub-Saharan norm, in-context training is vitally important:

> Kierkegaard...recommended "indirect" communication approaches that engage people's imaginations, such as through narrative, that "wound from behind" and help people to "discover" truth.... [S]tory telling and other appeals to the imagination are effective with many pre-Christian and post-Christian populations, and a sole reliance on direct propositional speaking is seldom as effective as it should be anywhere.[32]

Contextual approaches that are both biblical and prudent will be modeled and taught through both formal and informal means. We cannot continue to make the mistake of assuming our sub-Saharan training is adequate for North African realities. We must be willing to learn new approaches and forms without conceding orthodox belief and praxis.

> Bill White contends that changing one's *language* profoundly aids recovery.... Likewise, people in recovery need to shed the *symbols,* daily *rituals, music,* and role models that fuel the addictive lifestyle (like converts from primal religions who burn their fetishes when converting to Christianity), and replace them with the symbols, daily rituals, music, and role models that focus and empower recovery. One needs to say goodbye to the old *institutions,* that is, the "slippery places," and hang out at healthy, drug-free havens. Recovery involves acquiring a new oral *history* and a larger Story within which to understand one's life, and a new wisdom to guide one's life.[33]

Only as we learn from our context, and are willing to amend our presentation so that it is understandable, will we be able to present the gospel to Muslim Arabs in a way that is culturally acceptable and spiritually revolutionary. Only careful biblical training that is fleshed out in context can prepare our African missionaries to thrive in the difficult lands we are considering sending them to.

Let us covenant to be a missionary people who partner together in establishing a church-planting and Arabic-language center in North Africa for our multi-faceted missionary teams. Let this center be initially led by an experienced AGWM missionary couple, and let it be established and opened by August 1, 2013. Let us set the goal of having eight AAGA couples and eight AGWM couples enrolled in this center by that date.

**Partnering in Leadership**

Mission work in Africa has come full circle. We have moved from the paternalism of the colonial era to the partnership models that followed World War II. We now navigate the confusing and exciting channels of participation. Church and mission now have multiple partners and each chooses when and how to engage one another. Relationships are more fluid, multi-lateral, and fraternal. It no longer matters if you are black or white—or any combination of the two; what is now more important is your gifting, your capacity, and your spirit.

These exciting times, combined with the immense challenge of the Muslim world, and specifically the unengaged peoples of North Africa, necessitate that both missionary and national set aside past grievances and press forward to our preferred future. We must legitimately share leadership. If this means an American leads the team, let him be considered the leader, based not on his skin color but on his experience. If an African leads, let it be likewise, the content of his character determining his role.

Essential to leadership is the wisdom to know when to exit. "Church-planting missionaries…must ever anticipate the day when they can leave… [F]rom the earliest stages the Pauline Cycle points forward to missionary withdrawal—to the passing of the baton."[34] Let us commit to indigenous principles among the Muslim peoples we together reach, looking forward to the day when they assume leadership of their own, allowing us to move on to other unreached peoples.

Let us covenant to be a missionary people who are increasingly color blind, appointing missionaries to leadership based on competency and not on skin color. Let our leadership reflect this exciting age of voluntary participation, in that African and non-African together lead, and together follow. Let us leave behind the mistakes of the past and the awkwardness of the present to rejoice in mutual submission.

**Partnering in Sacrifice**

If we are to partner to send church-planting missionary teams to North Africa, we must do so in both faith and realism. Some of our missionaries will fail. Some fight with one another. Some will fall at the hands of angry Muslim men or mobs. We must, therefore, pre-decide that, when this happens, we will send more. The time to decide about deployment is not when some of our best have tragically been slain, but now in the clear-eyed, level emotion of simple obedience. God is calling us to take the gospel to these difficult lands and the deceived Muslim peoples of North Africa.

God is calling us to dwell where demons lurk and evil spirits linger. Let us be honest with ourselves. There will be great cost, tragedy, labor, and disappointment. Blood will be shed. Tears will flow. A price will be paid. If we together do this, let us do it agreeing to future costs, committed to paying all of them—no matter how painful, no matter who pays.

Part of the sacrifice required as we move forward together is the sacrifice of not knowing. We must commit to sending our missionaries into Muslim contexts not knowing if they will live, not knowing if they will survive, and not knowing if they will bear fruit that can be numerically counted or justified. We must be comfortable with an organic system that is not always well defined. J. Herbert Kane lucidly describes the balance between knowing (strategy) and Holy Spirit dependence (trust):

Did Paul have a missionary strategy? Some say yes; others say no. Much depends on the definition of strategy. If by strategy is meant a deliberate, well formulated, duly executed plan of action based on human observation and experience, then Paul had little or no strategy; but if we take the word to mean a flexible *modus operandi* developed under the guidance of the Holy Spirit and subject to His direction and control, then Paul did have a strategy.

Our problem today is that we live in an anthropocentric age. We imagine that nothing of consequence can be accomplished in the Lord's work without a good deal of ecclesiastical machinery—committees, conferences, workshops, seminars; whereas the early Christians depended less on human wisdom and expertise, more on divine initiative and guidance. It is obvious that they didn't do too badly. What the modern missionary movement needs above everything else is to get back to the missionary methods of the early church.[35]

The methods of the early church included embracing mystery and pain, joy and suffering, because Jesus is worth everything. Grains of wheat must not only be willing, but happy, to fall into the ground and die. Happy because otherwise they remain alone, but dying they produce much fruit.

Let us covenant to be a missionary people who live and die together with no reserves, no retreat, and no regrets. Let us understand that we send some of our missionaries to their deaths, and upon such agreement, covenant to send more when those we love witness their love and obedience to Christ by dying. We do so because Jesus is worth it, because Jesus is worth all things, and because for us to live is Christ and to die is gain.

## CONCLUSION

In the task of together taking the gospel, the good news of what God has done in Christ, to the whole world, I propose we start by turning our hearts and prayers to the unengaged Muslim peoples of Northern Africa. In summary, I today call for a commitment to the following recommendations:

1. Let us covenant to be a missionary people who are Spirit-led and data-informed. Let us believe that God can use data to help us understand the times and hear His voice in determining where we send our missionaries. Let the guiding questions for our missionary placement be, "Where does the church not exist?" and "What are we going to do about it?"

2. Let us covenant to be a missionary people who bear God's passion for the whole world, even as we allow Him to lead us to a priority and sequence of focus. Let our first focus be the unengaged Muslim peoples of Mauritania, Morocco, Algeria, Tunisia, Libya, Egypt, Northern Sudan, and Somalia.

3. Let us covenant to be a missionary people who together pray unceasingly for unreached peoples. Let us dedicate Friday as a day of prayer and fasting in all our churches. Let us appoint a prayer coordinator to the AAGA/WMC whose primary role is to travel the region and mobilize prayer for the Muslim peoples of Africa.

4. Let us covenant to be a missionary and Pentecostal people who humbly collaborate with other kingdom-minded workers who are ministering among unreached peoples. Let us pursue membership in the Vision 5:9 partnership, and encourage our missionaries in context to be a vital, contributing, leading part of every evangelical consortium that seeks to plant churches among unreached peoples. Let us pursue relationship with the emerging Assemblies of God fellowships in North Africa.

5. Let us covenant to be a missionary people who partner together to place multi-faceted church-planting teams in Mauritania, Morocco, Algeria, Tunisia, Libya, Egypt, Northern Sudan, and Somalia by 2015. Let eight AAGA-member churches fully support a catalytic missionary couple from each of their countries with adequate monthly support and a cash reserve for work needs. Each AAGA missionary couple will join with an AGWM couple to form eight church-planting teams in North Africa.

6. Let us covenant to be a missionary people who partner together in establishing businesses that can make a way for tentmaking missionaries to thrive in North Africa. Each AAGA country shall support one capable and mature missionary couple who will serve as way makers for others, with AGWM shouldering the responsibility for raising the investment capital that is needed for the success of the venture.

7. Let us covenant to be a missionary people who partner together in establishing a church-planting and Arabic-language center in North Africa for our multi-faceted missionary teams. Let this center be led by an experienced AGWM couple, and let it be established and opened by August 1, 2013. And let us set the goal of having eight AAGA couples and eight AGWM couples enrolled in this center by August of 2013.

8. Let us covenant to be a missionary people who are increasingly color blind, appointing missionaries to leadership based on competency and not on skin color. Let our leadership reflect this exciting age of voluntary participation in that African and non-African together lead and together follow. Let us leave behind the mistakes of the past and the awkwardness of the present to rejoice in mutual submission.

9. Let us covenant to be a missionary people who live and die together with no reserves, no retreat, and no regrets. Let us understand that we send some of our missionaries to their deaths, and upon such agreement, covenant to send more when those we love witness their love and obedience to Christ by dying. We do so because Jesus is worth it, because Jesus is worth all things, and because for us to live is Christ and to die is gain.

## ENDNOTES

[1] In December 5, 2010, edition of the *Pentecostal Evangel,* John Bueno, Executive Director of Assemblies of God World Missions (USA) wrote "Over the years some have criticized our missions methods. Many modern missiologists think we should be more deliberate in determining where our missionaries are sent. They believe we should place missionaries in areas of greatest need determined by studies, rather than allowing the Holy Spirit to guide them to their areas of service."

[2] Craig Ott and Harold A. Netland, *Globalizing Theology: Belief and Practice in an Era of World Christianity* (Grand Rapids, MI: Baker Academic, 2006), 228.

[3] Conversation with the author, December 10, 2011, at the Assemblies of God Theological Seminary, Springfield, MO, USA.

[4] People groups are delimited by four usual criteria: religion, culture, language and geography. If none of these barriers to the gospel exist, then that people is usually considered cohesive enough to be listed as unique.

[5] Essentially missiological breakthrough occurs when there are enough trained indigenous believers capable of reaching their own people.

[6] Engagement is defined as a missionary team in residence, committed to learning the local dialect with a long-term commitment to reach that people through a church-planting movement.

[7] Lausanne 3, Cape Town, October 2010, "Report."

[8] *Kenosis* theory, based on Philippians 2, informs us that God occasionally limits Himself. While Jesus often reached out to non-Jews, His primary pre-Pentecost mission was to the Jewish people. Jesus also did not heal everyone He could have healed (for instance the lame man at the temple) nor engage in every activity he could have (such as social action, condemning political injustice, etc). Therefore, we have the precedent and responsibility to limit ourselves to what the Spirit expressly asks us to do. Our obedience should be focused. We are not the answer to the whole world, and spreading ourselves too thinly, in the end, hurts our effectiveness. We have a stewardship responsibility to do what we do well.

[9] While it is true that Egypt has a sizable Christian population, including several evangelical denominations, and even an Assemblies of God church, it is also true that they have more Muslims than any other country in Africa. Egypt (along with Saudi Arabia) is one of the most important centers for Islamic thought and practice, thus making it strategically important for church-planting missionary endeavor.

[10] There are many Central Asian countries that once comprised the USSR that are not listed or considered here. They may be added, or it may be strategic to limit the Central Asian focus to the countries above.

[11] There are sizable populations of North African Muslims in France, Pakistani Muslims in England, and Turkish Muslims in Germany.

[12] Paul R. Gupta and Sherwood G. Lingenfelter, *Breaking Tradition to Accomplish Vision : Training Leaders for a Church-Planting Movement : A Case from India* (Winona Lake, IN: BMH Books, 2006), 98.

[13] Global Initiative is the new name for Center for Ministry to Muslims (CMM).

[14] Raymond J. Bakke, *A Theology as Big as the City* (Downers Grove, IL: InterVarsity Press, 1997), 138.

[15] Robert Webber, *Who Gets to Narrate the World?: Contending for the Christian Story in an Age of Rivals* (Downers Grove, IL: IVP Books, 2008), 84.

[16] *Stephen B. Bevans and Roger Schroeder, Constants in Context: A Theology of Mission for Today,* American Society of Missiology Series (Maryknoll, NY: Orbis Books, 2004), 45.

[17] Webber, 47.

[18] Statistics taken from the Vision 5:9 "Partnership Report," January 2011.

[19] Believer's from a Muslim background (BMB's) used to be referred to as Muslim background believers (MBB's). They prefer to accent "believer" rather than "Muslim" in their identity.

[20] For a thorough explanation of church planting in teams I recommend *Vision of the Possible* by Daniel Sinclair. For a biblical explanation of the "Pauline cycle of church planting," I recommend *Planting Churches Cross-culturally* by David Hesselgrave.

[21] Gupta and Lingenfelter, 188.

[22] Frontiers was founded by Greg Livingstone and birthed out of Arab World Ministries in the early 1980's.It has as one of its core pillars a commitment to church planting among Muslims in teams.

[23] The Live Dead initiative is the vision of Greg Beggs, AGWM Area Director for East Africa, Greg Beggs.

[24] The rationale for this and a suggested minimum amount is explained later in this paper under the heading, "Creative Access."

[25] George G. Hunter, *The Celtic Way of Evangelism: How Christianity Can Reach the West—Again* (Nashville, TN: Abingdon Press, 2000), 20.

[26] Ibid., 28.

[27] Sometimes this has been a small business grant, sometimes it has been a practical tool like a milk cow or work donkey. It has always been modest and required steady industry on the part of the recipient.

[28] Gupta and Lingenfelter, 119.

[29] Bakke, 110.

[30] Gupta and Lingenfelter, 16.

[31] Ibid., 23.

[32] Hunter, 62.

[33] Ibid., 103.

[34] David J. Hesselgrave, *Planting Churches Cross-Culturally: North America and Beyond,* 2nd ed. (Grand Rapids, MI: Baker Books, 2000), 283.

[35] Ibid., 43.

# Planting Churches among Unreached Peoples: A Response to the Paper by Dick Brogden

UCHECHUKWU AMA

INTRODUCTION

The strategy paper presented by Dick Brogden on "Planting Churches among Unreached Peoples in Partnership with the AAGA World Missions Commission" is as classical as it is timely. He first traced the historical antecedent of the American Pentecostal missions movement to South America, occasioned by World War II, to the Sudan Interior Missions based in Nigeria. He drew attention to the critical information and inspiration provided by four major missionary research agencies that have helped the church today with data and basic information on the current state of world evangelization. These agencies are the *World Encyclopedia,* the AD2000 and Beyond Movement, the International Missions Board of the Southern Baptist Convention (US) and the Ethnologue of SIL.

Brogden's document addressed head on the need of the hour, and made a passionate appeal for the Africa Assemblies of God Alliance (AAGA) to adopt seven key proposals that he believes will help them, as part of the "Missional People of God," to complete the work of evangelizing the continent. Brogden thus focused on the following key issues: (1) *Task:* redefining our approach to the task, calling for prioritization and sequence of focus; (2) *Synergy:* partnership in critical areas of prayer, collaboration, teams, creative access, training, leadership, and sacrifice; (3) *Focus:* refocusing ourselves on the Muslim world, particularly in North Africa, as the major challenge; (4) *Deployment:* deploying missionary teams in creative access initiatives that would make room for more workers; (5) *Training Center:* the need for an Arabic-language Training Center to adequately address the growing need to reach the Arab world; (6) *MOU:* the necessity to develop a "Memorandum of Understanding" to guide our strategic partnerships; and (7) *Martyrdom:* preparing the church for the likelihood of post-martyrdom providence.

These are indeed key considerations for church planting in North Africa. There are, however, in my opinion, other critical issues that must be addressed. In the following response, I have tried to first draw attention to the need to examine all of the challenges of the Africa harvest before zeroing in on any one particular area. I have also tried to list what I believe to be the first fifteen major missional challenges for the Africa AG, leaving others for future discussion. Some of these challenges, if neglected, could have a negative impact on Brogden's proposals.

In this context I call on the Consultation to marshal a massive movement of the AAGA family of churches towards an unprecedented missionary thrust, leveraging AAGA's declaration of the Decade of Pentecost (2010-2020) and the ongoing activities of the Acts in Africa Initiative led by Dr. Denzil R. Miller. Missionary thrust of any magnitude is possible only in the power of the Holy Spirit. The church must therefore return to its intrinsic connection with the person, presence, and power of the Holy Spirit to complete the task.

## THE CONSULTATION

**A Timely Call**

When Dr. Enson Lwesya, chairman of the World Missions Commission of the Africa Assemblies of God Alliance (AAGA/WMC), first wrote to stakeholders about the forthcoming Pentecostal Missions Consultation, I sensed that it was indeed timely and God-inspired. I believe this because of my awareness of three realities:

First, the AAGA/WMC since its inception in 1991 has not had a clear action plan complete with implementation processes to actualize the task of evangelization. Throughout the Decade of Harvest of the 1990's, the focus of the Commission was centered on coordinating what the various member national churches were doing in missions rather than serving as a catalytic agent in the process. During the quadrennial sessions of the AAGA General Assembly, we listened to what the brethren, through the power of the Holy Spirit, were doing in such places as Malawi, Kenya, Tanzania, and Nigeria. At the time, the AAGA leadership came from these countries. We thus had the privilege of hearing their testimonies.

Second, I saw the coming Consultation to be reminiscent of what happened twelve years ago in August of 1999 during the Eleventh Hour Institute (EHI) that took place in Lilongwe, Malawi. Unfortunately, as Brogden noted, in many cases the EHI resulted mostly in rhetoric. Nevertheless, the objective, packaging, and delivery of the EHI and the continental follow-up were productive. To me this Consultation is a revisiting of the issue of Africa's role in reaching the nations with the gospel. So I have looked forward to it with both nostalgia and anticipation.

Third, I see this Consultation as divinely timed to coincide with the launch of AAGA's Decade of Pentecost. What the EHI was to the Decade of Harvest, this Consultation can be for the Decade of Pentecost. This is no coincidence. Rather I see the Holy Spirit gathering the leadership of the Africa AG missionary movement to help generate the needed momentum for the task ahead.

With these things in mind, I am deeply touched by the passion with which Brogden has written his document urging the church in Africa to head north. He poignantly reminds us of what Alan R. Johnson said, "We cannot pretend to not know what we know." Brogden's words seemed to me to be prophetic, as the Arabic revolution began in Tunisia, spread to Egypt, then to Bahrain, and finally to Libya until it engulfed the North Africa region, and, by extension, to the entire Arabic world. I, therefore, consider our gathering here to be a fulfillment of the prophecy that God would someday make "a highway in Egypt" (Isa. 19:23) which He has stretched throughout North Africa and beyond.

At the recent World Assemblies of God Congress in Chennai, India, held in February of this year, the global AG family was urged to move "Forward." One purpose that congress may have served is the ignition of a greater passion for the church in Africa and the world to come together in powerful synergy prompting the kind of partnerships that Brogden has referred to in his paper. Currently AAGA is a loosely-knit fraternity and, therefore, is not constitutionally positioned to provide such momentum. Since it has no control over its member churches, it cannot enforce regulations or resolutions. It merely depends on the goodwill of the leaders of its constituent member churches and organizations to garner sufficient support to address the missional challenges in the continent. Because such goodwill is often a scarce commodity, the organization lacks the motive power or political clout required to provide the kind of leadership that is needed. This is one reason why we have responded to crises very slowly, even when our churches were burned and our brethren were killed in places like Rwanda, the Democratic Republic of Congo, Nigeria, and Cote d'Ivoire. We have no means to garner the kind of emergency response needed to aid the victims of such socio-political conflicts, our own brothers and sisters in Christ with whom we share the hope of eternal life.

This demonstrates why we must not leave this place to again face the setbacks experienced by the good proposals of the 1999 EHI in Lilongwe. Its impact was mitigated because much of the momentum created by godly men and seasoned missionaries, such as our late brother, Dr. John V. York, and our current AAGA chairman, Dr. Lazarus Chakwera, waned soon after it was created. This is why we are here again to say, "Yes, we can!" We can work together; we can partner together to fulfill the primary task the Lord of the Harvest has placed on our shoulders.

**Key Issues**

Three key issues addressed in this paper are church planting, unreached peoples (especially among Muslims), and strategic partnerships. While appreciating a passion for reaching the unreached, we should not see "planting churches" as a project of greater importance than reaching the hearts of the people with the love of Christ. If we simply count the number of churches we have planted as being equivalent to completing our missionary task, we will, in my opinion, be getting it wrong. First, it is possible that the churches we plant may be completely alien to the culture of the local people and, therefore, largely irrelevant to their context. Second, a church may be planted among the people that is only concerned with "spiritual matters" and is insensitive to the suffering of the people, who themselves see the church primarily as an agent of social change providing holistic succor to their felt needs. And yet, because the church planters saw it differently, the church is perceived as a nuisance rather than as a blessing to the people.

Third, when we just plant a church without simultaneously providing an effective discipleship program, the members of the new church quickly lose touch with spiritual realities associated with the maintenance of their spiritual lives. The church then begins to slowly die, and, what Paul referred to as "ravaging wolves," come in and sweep them away (cf. Acts 20:29). We should learn from history. The problem we may have to address, therefore, is, "What kind of church do we intend to plant among the Muslims?" It will definitely be different from the type we would plant in New York City, Lagos, or Nairobi. While it is good to use indigenous church principles as our guide, the twenty-first century church must be more than just self-propagating, self-governing and self-supporting.

We must now contextualize this venerated church-planting paradigm and the model it promotes. This is necessary because the original context of this missionary strategy is fast becoming abused, and may even be moribund in the context of contemporary African missions. One reason this is true is because the indigenous model was originally created to help western missionaries empower indigenous peoples to develop the capacity to evangelize their own people, to be financially non-dependent, and to be able to lead themselves. However, through the years a number changes have taken place.

For instance, the people are, in many cases, incapable of independently evangelizing peoples beyond their own. They need to enter into strategic partnerships such as the ones Brogden is positing for North Africa. This seems to me to be a perfect match. This partnership idea flows from what is understood to be the indigenous principle. The indigenous church-planting principle's emphasis on "self" was relevant for the western missionaries and their senders, because they had the good intention of developing the fledgling churches into mature, self-reliant churches. Sadly, today those toddlers have not grown teeth and become strong.

Indeed, in some cases, they now even bite the hand that once fed them. Worse still, in some cases they have redefined the word "self" to mean "selfish." These churches have become "selfish-propagating," no more looking beyond their immediate gospel influence; "selfish-supporting," no more helping sister national churches, even when their churches are being burned and members are being murdered in uprisings; and "selfish-governing," grasping for power and refusing to allow others outside their own ethnic group access to power. They even deny apostolic influence to the very men and women who have labored among them to establish the church.

While the indigenous principles are useful, we must remember that they are not inspired Scripture, and can, therefore, be improved upon. My concern is that, when understood and applied out of their original context, the indigenous principles fall short of properly promoting the place of the Holy Spirit in the mission of God. To a later generation of Africa leaders, a Spirit-centered mission has become self-centered. What we need to pass on to the next generation of Africa leaders, therefore, is not an ambiguous concept of indigeniety, but a clear, biblically-based missiological philosophy that recognizes the power of the Holy Spirit in promoting and sustaining the harvest. We must move from a self-driven to a *Spirit-driven* missional praxis. If that was what the previous strategy was meant to achieve, it did not clearly state so. Today we suffer the burden of limiting our gospel influence to where our self—or selfish—interests stop. This is a serious matter.

Further, the Melvin Hodges of the blessed memory did not intend to promote an "all generations" rule of the thumb. He simply wrote what the Spirit directed him to write for the kind and nature of the work of his time. He did not, as I have stated, write a biblical script for all times and places. He, rather, wrote on strategic principles which worked for the western missionaries during and soon after World War II.

I am encouraged by the 2011 World Assemblies of God Congress' clarion call, "FORWARD 20/20." But let us go beyond mere declaration. Like God warned Moses, we have dwelt around this mountain for too long. It is time to move forward. God, indeed, led the Israelites unto that mountain, but He did not intend for them to remain there. This is an analogy for our time. The world is now a global village, symbiotically interconnected by rapid trends in information technology. Church planting and soul winning can now be done intercontinentally through the Internet. Unreached peoples now have access to the truth that we have been discussing in conferences year after year. The revolution that is now occurring in the Arabic world was not triggered by practitioners of indigenous church-planting principles, but by the younger generation, heavily exposed to online social networking through the social media, such as Facebook and Twitter on one hand, and cable network news on the other. Through these media and other global sources they came to understand their right to freedom, and they simultaneously decided to bring a change at all cost. That is the age we are living in today.

Thank God for our AAGA leadership and AG families who have been praying for the Muslims of North Africa. To them this revolution is good news! They know that what is happening is an answer to their prayers. Yet the question remains, "How many of us are ready to mobilize our national churches to head to Libya, Egypt, Tunisia, Algeria, Morocco, Sudan, or elsewhere in North Africa?" The disappointing and disturbing fact is that this scenario is not even on most of our agendas. Few of us have even thought about it. Unfortunately, many of us are preoccupied with other things, such as church politics and acquiring more degrees and titles. Why are we so indifferent? In light of these issues this conference is timely and strategic.

It seems to me that the first challenge of this conference is to commit to revisit, and possibly to rewrite, our present vision and mission statements to fit into the kind of missionary enterprise the Lord is calling us to. To do this we should first, through the contextualization process, deconstruct our understanding of the indigenous principle so that we will be released towards a more synergetic commitment that will sustain our proposed partnership. This deconstruction should not in any way devalue the concept, since, as a strategy, it has served its purpose well, and its purpose remains a valuable legacy. Neither should we confine it to the archives of missionary history. We should, rather, use it as a springboard to develop a more practical strategy in the context of our present task.

I therefore beg to differ with others in supporting the idea that this process should continue to mill out more "self" concepts, such as "self-theologizing" or "self-missionizing," as was discussed in the 1999 EHI in Malawi. The more "selfs" we develop, the deeper we descend into the abyss of missional stagnation that we are trying, with the Spirit's help, to lift ourselves out of. What we must now think about a *Spirit-driven* missional praxis.

We would thus do well to get back to where it all began. What happened in the church in Syrian Antioch (Acts 13:1-4) was not a self-driven strategy, it was Spirit-driven strategy. Let us take it from there. In his book, *The Move of the Holy Spirit in the 10/40 Window,* Luis Bush, International Director of the AD2000 and Beyond Movement, noted that what was happening among the predominantly Islamic Arab world, the Buddhists of China, the Hindus of India, and the animists of South Asia, all living in the 10/40 Window, was the move of the Spirit, and not the result of applying humanly-devised principles nor strategies. Such thinking promises to be more inspiring and enduring for our next generation of African leaders.

This is why the Acts 1:8 Conferences led by the Acts in Africa Initiative are setting the pace and laying the needed foundation to bring the church back to where it all began. We fear that self-theologizing will not only open the door to syncretism, it will also disjoint what really holds us together—sound biblical doctrine. Similarly, self-missionizing, whatever that means, threatens to narrow our thinking to home-grown missionary enterprises that have little or no global application. Consequently, missionaries called and developed under such environments are in danger of being parochial rather than global in orientation and reach. They could, by default, give the Great Commission and all of its mandates, only lip service in the context of what they perceive, or want, missions to be.

## CRITICAL REVIEW

In the light of the foregoing, allow me to critically review what Dick Brogden has recommended to this Consultation. In his paper he described how the outbreak of World War II in Europe led to the redeployment of Africa- and Asia-bound US Assemblies of God missionaries to Latin America. At that point in history large-scale deployment of missionaries to Latin America was not the intention AG Division of Foreign Missions. However, either by an accident of history, or by the providential will of the Spirit, they were diverted away from their originally-intended target people. Brogden wonders if the German naval blockade of the Atlantic Ocean was an accident of history or an act of God. My take on this situation is that it was truly a move of the Spirit to redeploy American AG missionaries to Latin America, and not an accident of history, nor a hindrance of Satan.

Brogden later discussed the issue of unreached peoples and the need for the church and its leadership to respect the significance of the data that has been generated by missions researchers and the institutions over the years towards world evangelization. The concept of unreached peoples which was promoted by research experts such as Ralph Winter and others in the AD2000 and Beyond Movement has changed the face of missiological thinking and practice.

Brogden contends that such data helps to bring clarity and direction to the task, clarity which the church cannot afford to ignore. Moreover, Brogden affirms that the Holy Spirit can, and does, use this information to enable the church to accomplish the task of world evangelization. He warns that our failure to admit this may also be our failure to obey the Spirit. He thus challenges the resistance by Pentecostals to such data, and their defensive posture to the same. He even asserts that "some of our resistance to data is actually resistance to the Holy Spirit." He cautions us Pentecostals to not make the mistake of blaming the Holy Spirit for our "disproportionate deployment" of human and fiscal resources away from unreached peoples of the world.

**Main Thrust**

The main thrust of Brogden's paper concerns planting churches among the Muslims of North Africa. He further focuses on the development of strategic partnerships within the AAGA/WMC and the Assemblies of God World Missions (US) that will be required to move forward from here. He postulates that our church-planting efforts in North Africa should move forward in strategic sequential steps targeting the unengaged Muslims of the region. In the area of partnerships, he cites seven critical areas which will require strategic partnering: (1) partnering in prayer, (2) partnering in collaboration, (3) partnering in teams, (4) partnering in creative access, (5) partnering in training, (6) partnering in leadership, and (7) partnering in sacrifice.

RESPONSE

**General Response**

Truly, the ways of the Lord are past finding out (Rom. 11:33). It is surprising to discover that God used Methodist missionaries led by John Perkins who arrived in Liberia on December 25, 1908, some six years before the US Assemblies of God was founded in 1914, to open the first local Assemblies of God church in Africa. It is equally surprising that in Nigeria in 1934 the largest AG national church in Africa was started by members of the Faith Tabernacle Church who were tired of mediocrity in the faith. The determination of those few people to seek after God and hold unto the truth of His word has now matured into a national church of more than three million members meeting in 15,000 congregations throughout Nigeria. It was later that the US church was contacted and sent a missionary to Nigeria. God's ways are different from our ways. The promptings of the Holy Spirit and His agenda are different also.

A new chapter in African missions is about to unfold, and God has gathered us here to witness it first hand—the birth of a new AG missionary movement in Africa, empowered by the Holy Spirit to complete the task of evangelizing the continent and beyond before the soon-coming of Christ our Lord.

**Historical Review**

At the beginning of the Decade of Harvest of the 1990s, AAGA leaders gathered to find ways to evangelize Africa. At the time they did not intend to form an alliance. What led to the formation of the Alliance was the need for a structure to coordinate the evangelistic and church-planting efforts of the various national churches during the Decade of Harvest (1990-2000). The Spirit prompted the formation of AAGA to help provide impetus to the harvest. National and continental goals for church planting, ministerial training, and soul winning were set.

Later, in 1991, the World Missions Commission was formed with the Rev. Lazarus Chakwera, General Superintendent of the Assemblies of God in Malawi, representing Southern Africa; the Rev. Jean Baptist Sawadago, Missions Director of the Burkina Faso AG, representing West Africa, and the Rev. Uche Ama, Nigerian Decade of Harvest Research Coordinator representing Central Africa; and the Rev. Scott Hanson, US missionary to Tanzania, representing East Africa. These four men along with the US Area Directors also served as members of the International Committee for Emerging Missions and Unreached People formed in London. The name of this organization was later changed to the World Assemblies of God Fellowship Missions Commission. More recently Dr. Enson Lwesya has been appointed as Chairman and of the AAGA/WMC with Dr. Chakwera serving as AAGA Chairman. Rev. Edward Chitsonga now serves as the Southern Africa Missions Representative. The WMC has been mandated to set up the structure and develop and promote policies that will assist national churches in pursuing their missionary goals. I perceive this to be more that just a supervisory role; it is a leadership role; the mandate is strong.

## SWOT ANALYSIS

Before the AAGA/WMC can make a firm decision on Brogden's proposal, it is important that we take an inward look at our efforts thus far as an agency of the Alliance missionary enterprise, and then redefine and clarify our roles in that context. In other words, let us examine the strengths, weaknesses, opportunities, and threats (SWOT) that have brought the Commission to where it is today. We also need to examine whether the Commission has the necessary authority and resources to support Brogden's proposals, since at present we have no such mandate from the AAGA General Assembly. Put another way, what is the extent of our authority?

**Strengths**

The strength of the Commission rests in its mandate given by the Alliance itself. If the Alliance lacks strength to mobilize its members, then the Commission is weakened, since the strength of the Commission cannot exceed that of the body that set it up. Thus the strength of the Commission to move Assemblies of God in Africa forward lies squarely with the Alliance itself. It does appear, however, that the Commission can derive further strength from within if it develops instruments of operation which can then be ratified by the AAGA leadership. These instruments could include a well-articulated constitution, an action plan for the Decade of Pentecost (2010-2020), a creative operational system with an operational base, and the appointment of a full-time executive director or secretary.

**Weaknesses**

Our weakness lies in the fact that, though good fellowship does from time to time exist among some of the AAGA leaders and between certain national leaders, such a privilege has yet to be extended to people at the grassroots. For example, a world-class, AAGA-sponsored congress has never been attempted. Perhaps we are yet to see ourselves as one people with one purpose and one task. Our leaders may help us here. They can take note of the longing for greater connection that exists in the hearts of many of our constituent members. While the great challenges of the multi-lingual and multi-cultural stratification of our continent truly exist, the Commission should, nevertheless, resolve to strengthen our relational capabilities. This should be done, not necessarily with more conferences, but by engaging in practical missional exposure to one another, and through activities of critical concern to our sister AG national churches. One example of this is the work the AG Nigeria (which is Anglophone) is doing in Gabon (which is Francophone) through the REAP Project of the Central Africa Assemblies of God Alliance (CAAGA). Another is the merger that took place in 2007 in Libreville between Nigerian missionary congregations in Gabon and the Gabonese AG. In this merger five existing Nigerian congregations were formally handed over to the Gabon AG church.

## Opportunities

The opportunities we have today include those provided by the Decade of Harvest, the Eleventh Hour Institute, AG Care, the AAGA Emergency Relief Agency, Pan Africa Theological Seminary, and other AG theological institutions throughout Africa. They also include AAGA's Decade of Pentecost campaign and the Acts 1:8 Conferences and Schools of the Spirit being conducted throughout Africa by the Acts in Africa Initiative. A host of other networks, conferences, consultations, and international forums are also available. We should explore these and other opportunities for fellowship and collaboration. We also possess the ability to create other strategic opportunities, such as the one Brogden has proposed.

## Threats

Our missional success also faces certain threats. These threats include the following:

1. *Data Base.* Our inabilities to effectively generate, collate, process, and share current accurate information from our own database poses one threat to our missional success. This information should reflect the progress

we are making on a real-time basis. We need to know what we have done, what we are doing, and what we plan to do. For a start, even Twitter or a professionally-managed and restricted Facebook account could serve as a collaborative tool. In order words, our dependence on external information gathering and sharing systems, like that of the Southern Baptists and others, which, in some cases, are quite inaccurate, can be a minus for the Alliance and its networks, including the Commission.

2. *Monitoring System.* Our inability to provide a monitoring system for our missionary and church-planting activities further serves to mitigate our collective effectiveness towards the task. Churches and missionaries in the field need to be able to report their progress back to their sending bases and ultimately to the continental AG family. This information could then be used as a mobilization tool towards enhanced missional effectiveness.

3. *Operational Base.* Our inability to have an operational base or central office charged with responsibility of coordinating or implementing the decisions of the AAGA/WMC represents yet another threat to effective progress. Unfortunately, what we have now is a makeshift, unfunded, and unstaffed operation that depends solely on the goodwill of our leaders resulting in intermittent and inconsistent function.

4. *Support Base.* Our inability to have a credible and adequate financial budget and support base that can be used to implement and sustain our resolutions represents another serious threat to progress. "No one should go to war at his own expense" (cf. 1 Cor. 9:7), and yet, that is just what we are attempting to do. Depending on the goodwill of the leaders of hosting national churches to sponsor programs of the Commission, including this conference, the work does not get done. Who pays the bills, not just for this conference, but for the ongoing projects and programs that should follow?

5. *Communications.* Finally, our inability to effectively communicate with the grassroots and have corresponding feedback from AAGA leaders, pastors, members, and other stakeholders, is mitigating our efforts to accomplish anything of great significance. And it will remain so, unless these critical issues are addressed and remedied.

## A Wake-up Call

The current revolution in the Arabic world, and the prophetic significance of these events, in my opinion, constitute a wake-up call to the church, declaring to us that "the fields are ripe for harvest" (John 4:35). The Lord of the Harvest is shaking up those nations that, before now, were locked up against the gospel. We must prayerfully seek the Spirit's answers to such questions as, "What is God telling us by these simultaneous revolts of the younger generation against the autocratic rule in the Arabic world?" and "Why are these same young people so resistant to the status quo?" and "Why are they succeeding in their efforts, though at a great price?" What is happening in the Arabic world is a wake up call for kingdom purpose. We cannot continue to pray, "Lord, open the doors to the Islamic world," for that door, which has been closed since the eighth century, is now being opened in our generation. Truly, Brogden's paper serves as yet another wake-up call to the African church. Do we have the will to obediently respond?

## Brogden's Proposal

As I understand it, Brother Brogden recommended the following strategies:

1. We should focus our church-planting efforts on the Muslims in North Africa by prioritizing, allocating, and strategizing in definite steps based on a predetermined time-line.

2. We should enter into strategic partnerships through prayer, collaboration, and teams employing creative access in business, manpower, and leadership development.

3. We should build our future concept of mobilization, sensitization, and deployment of laborers on the understanding that they may pay the supreme prize of martyrdom. When this happens, the church must have the resilience, determination, and the logistical commitment to replace these "heroes of faith" without giving in to despondency.

## Further Recommendations

While Brogden's' proposal is indeed timely and strategic, he seems to have overlooked certain continental challenges of the African harvest that must be considered before zeroing in exclusively on the challenges of the Islamic nations of North Africa. While I agree that looking at unreached people groups through the lens of religious blocs, especially the Islamic blocs of North Africa, can be a bit overwhelming, looking at them through the lens of their socio-economic, cultural, and political affinities can serve a wider purpose. The revolutions that are occurring in North Africa and the Middle East are not being fueled primarily by the forces of religious affinity. Rather, the people are simply fed up with their economic and socio-political conditions and are seeking change, change which they believe democracy may provide them.

If we go to North Africa and say to them, "Hey, you are Muslims and we are Christians, and we have come to spread our religion among you," then we should be ready to dig our own graves, since martyrdom will inevitably be our reward. But if we identify with their socio-economic or political yearnings, and then wisely offer solutions to their heart-felt longings in the gospel of the kingdom, then our mission is more likely to bear fruit. These Muslims, however, are not only found in North Africa. There are, in fact, more Muslims living south of the Sahara than north. Therefore, we should examine the entire continent to see how ripe the fields are for harvest. Let us, therefore, see all of the challenges posed by the African harvest, and then, under the Spirit's guidance, determine where best to deploy our workers. We should do the one without neglecting the other.

Allow me now to address two of our greatest immediate challenges, and leave the rest to a soon-coming quarterly publication, the *Acts 1:8 International Magazine*.

## THE CHALLENGES OF AFRICA HARVEST

### Islamic Ideological Expansion in Africa

The 2010 edition of *Operation World* reveals that the Islamic communities constitute 41.47% of the more than one billion persons living in Africa, and they are growing at an annual rate of 2.4%. This means that every day in Africa about 28,165 persons are added to the Islamic religion either through birth or conversion. Annually, this amounts to more than one million souls. By extension, every second eight new Muslims exist in Africa! Citing the Islamic jihadists of Somalia, northern Nigeria and northeastern Kenya, *Operation World* notes that in Africa Islam is often characterized by extreme violence. We are, therefore, compelled to study and develop strategies to address and resist the continued violence occasioned by Islamic expansion on the continent. Other than the church, no other institution, including the UN, can effectively address this issue. Only the church, through the power of the gospel, the power of the Spirit, and the life of Christ we present to them, has God's mandate to mitigate the excesses of the "sons of Ishmael."

**Unreached Peoples throughout All of Africa**

Africa's Muslims live in many different people groups. According to the Joshua Project, of the unreached peoples of Central and West Africa, 112 are Islamic with a total population of about 21 million persons. Of these, 87 are completely unreached with the gospel. Similarly, in East and Southern Africa, there are 32 unreached Islamic people groups amounting to 16.5 million individuals. Further, there are several key unreached people groups that cut across several predominantly Islamic countries. These groups have a history of affecting the lives of other Muslims on the continent. These particular mega-people groups should be on our priority list. They include the Arabs and Berbers of North of Africa, numbering 210 million and 18 million people respectively. These Arabic peoples reside in countries from Mauritania in the West to Egypt in the East. They include 2.5 million Tuaregs and 32.4 million Hausas in Nigeria and other countries. In Kenya, for example, there live 25 unreached Islamic people groups totaling 4.2 million people. Only five of these groups—less than 20%—have had any form of gospel engagement.

The Kanuri people of Nigeria, numbering 6.9 million people, can serve as a case study. Their history of expansion and settlement dates back to the seventh century A.D. They have now spread into Niger, Chad, Cameroon, and even parts of Libya. Another important group is the nomadic Fulanis (Fulbes). They are a highly mobile people, and their religion has influenced the entire region, including North, West, and Central Africa. This mega-group, also called Fula (French), is the most dominant in the region. Their influence extends across Mauritania, Senegal, The Gambia, Guinea Bissau, Guinea, Mali, Burkina Faso, Sierra Leone, Liberia, Cote d'Ivoire, Ghana, Togo, Benin, Nigeria, Niger, Chad, Central African Republic, Cameroon, and Northern Sudan. They are the major agent for the spread of Islam in the region. We need to target them. Other challenges that must be factored in our efforts to evangelize Africa include the following,

- Growing mega-cities without adequate a gospel presence by the AG.
- Hunger and lack of effort towards food security.
- Illiteracy and poor educational structure.
- Bible translations needed among the complex mix of the 3200 ethno-linguistic indigenous groups.
- Drug abuse, child abuse, and the trafficking of young women.
- The ravages of HIV/AIDS, malaria, and tuberculosis.
- Syncretism and nominalism.
- Ethnic nationalism and conflicts.
- Youth restiveness, cultism, and occultism in the universities.
- Poor and "selfish" indigenous church-planting principles and strategies.
- Poverty and a declining socio-economic future for many Africans.
- Decaying or non-existent infrastructure.
- Rape on democracy and good governance, greed, and corruption.

## WHAT IS NEEDED TO MOVE FORWARD

**Strong Structures and Institutions**

During his recent visit to Accra, Ghana, President Barack Obama stated that what Africa needs to survive is not stronger men, but stronger structures and institutions. Today, as we look at the task before us, we could confidently repeat this assertion for the Africa Assemblies of God. Our greatest need is not great theologians, politicians, or men of great oratory skills. Our greatest need to accomplish the task is strong institutions and structures that will outlive our great men and provide us with an effective operational foundation for the next generation of missional leaders. Such structures include missionary-oriented Bible colleges with task-oriented curricula. These structures must include missions departments staffed by committed individuals who have a genuine calling for the task. We should further ensure that these structures and institutions meet pre-defined standards for quality assurance. This commission could help to define such standards.

**Clarifying the Task**

As we enter this Decade of Pentecost, we need to seriously evaluate the missional data we collect from non-Pentecostal sources concerning those who are wrongly classified as "reached" or "unreached." In some parts of Africa, members of quasi-Christian cults have been classified as "reached" by the gospel. This has at times included certain so-called "evangelical" groups whose deacons, elders, and even ministers participate in occultic practices. What, then, do we mean from a Pentecostal missiological perspective when we say a community of people has been reached with the gospel? Unfortunately, it is the non-Pentecostals who provide the definitions we use in assessing Pentecostal activities.

For example, at the recent Lausanne Conference in Cape Town some of my colleagues from the non-Pentecostal evangelical tradition had no understanding of the traditional Pentecostal position concerning what it means to be baptized in the Holy Spirit. And yet, these are the very ones who are informing us about who is "reached" and "unreached," and from where we measure progress in fulfilling the Great Commission. We need clarification in this area from a clear Pentecostal perspective. Such an endeavor may result in the reclassification of some peoples on the Joshua Project list from "reached" to "unreached."

**Strategic Partnership**

In our Africa Assemblies we sorely need to develop grounds for synergy among the national churches in the AAGA family. "Can two walk together unless they agree?" (Amos 3:3), and even when they do agree, can they work effectively together unless they are empowered by the Holy Spirit (Acts 1:8)? Sadly, the few AAGA leadership meetings that we have conducted have failed to relate to the grassroots. I recommend that we consider a world-class conference in the Africa AG that will involve the entire grassroots leadership of the church. It could be a conference much like Cape Town 2010 sponsored by the Lausanne Committee for World Evangelization or the conference being planned by the Movement for Africa National Initiative in Abuja, Nigeria, in September. At such a world-class conference we could expose our ministers and lay leaders to the opportunities that we, as a great African AG family, have to evangelize this continent and beyond. The AAGA/WMC Chairman, Dr. Enson Lwesya has spoken of such a continent-wide conference as a follow up of this Consultation. This idea should move beyond wishing and rhetoric to reality.

In order to create the needed impact, such an effort would require collaboration and support from the global AG family. Some leaders and members from poor countries and families may need to be sponsored. Besides conferences, we need to promote partnership as an ongoing lifestyle for the church. This initiative may or may not require a resolution of the AAGA leadership; however, we must start from somewhere. Two programs with which I have been connected that have succeeded because we synergized together are the Decade of Harvest and the REAP Project.

During the Decade of Harvest (1990-2000) the Assemblies of God Nigeria paired churches and allocated them to places outside their immediate domains of gospel influence, while, at the same time, getting the leaders of the churches to endorse the cause. By doing this we were able to penetrate more than fifty new people groups in Nigeria. When the Central Africa Assemblies of God Alliance (CAAGA) under the REAP Project (Rapid Evangelization of Africa Peoples) launched Mission Gabon, the Missions Department of CAAGA, with the support of the Executive Committee, decided to plant 22 new churches among the most needy people groups of Gabon. The AG Nigeria boldly took as its share nine churches. Other national churches took on three, two, or one church to plant. The project is working and churches are being planted in Gabon.

**Communication and Information Sharing**

Further, the Africa AG needs to develop and utilize information technology for effective communication of the gospel of the kingdom and for information sharing. No serious business today would think of functioning without the support of information technology. Likewise, kingdom business must be given the technological advantage provided by the Internet and other communication media. Someone has said, "Technology will not evangelize Africa, the Holy Spirit will." I agree! However, when such statements are made in strategic conferences, they inadvertently tend to weaken the resolve of the participants to ask the Holy Spirit to provide the technological tools needed to more effectively leverage the work. Just as we use the technology of automobiles and airplanes to help evangelize the world, we must also use the information technology at our fingertips. Did not each of us receive e-mails inviting us to this gathering and informing us of its progress? Likely, most of us will check our e-mails today and listen to cable television news to find out what is happening in the world. We need to exploit these and other technological tools to reach the nations with the gospel. We need to mobilize and train technocrats to address this critical issue. The Africa AG needs to launch a continent-wide television network. We need to own a dynamic state-of-the-art web portal, with high content management in order to synergize and share information and inspiration.

**Other Issues**

Other issues that need to be addressed include the following:

- Reexamining our current training philosophy and reconstructing our Bible school curricula and pedagogy for the greater task-oriented missional mobilization and training required by the Decade of Pentecost goals and initiatives.
- Initiating business developments and social actions aimed at developing "business as missions" initiatives.
- Adopting and expanding Dick Brogden's proposals to include non-Muslim challenges.
- Developing a holistic action plan for missions, incorporating and "Pentecostalizing" the philosophy of the 2010 Lausanne Conference, Commitment 2010, calling for real commitment.

- Coordinating the AAGA leadership and networks to endorse, commit themselves to, and implement an action plan in a special session specifically called to address that issue.
- Building an International Missions Center to efficiently coordinate the entire effort.
- Encouraging effective print and digital publications and information networks for grassroots mobilization.
- Inspiring and releasing the young people and lay people towards a continental network.
- Reviewing the political processes in the leadership structures and development of Africa AG.
- Incorporating the Decade of Pentecost into the mega-action-plan and develop study groups for strategic support and advice on each issue.

## CONCLUSION

In summary, I largely concur with the spirit and thrust of Dick Brogden's proposal, believing that it is both timely and strategic. However, before we zero exclusively in on just one missional challenge in Africa, it is important that we take a general look at all of the challenges. We must thoroughly understand any decision before we implement it. This will require dealing with issues within and without the AAGA family that may work against its success. This explains why my response is broader than Brogden's original proposal. If we embark on a mega-program like the one Brogden is proposing, it will require that the leadership of AAGA, as well as its constituent member churches, join together to support the initiative. As we, during this momentous Decade of Pentecost, in the Spirit's power, seek to "put our AG house in order," I am confident that we will leave this Consultation ready to go!

*Planting Churches Among Unreached Peoples: a Response*

# Planting Churches among Unreached Peoples: A Review of the Paper by Dick Brogden

ANDREW MKWAILA

### INTRODUCTION

Dick Brogden lays a missiological foundation for his proposals by arguing that as Pentecostals our understanding of the Spirit's leading in our missionary action must incorporate a consideration of data on unreached people. The data itself is clear: 300 million Muslims in Africa compel the AAGA to pay attention to the Holy Spirit's concern for the Muslim Unreached People Groups (MUPGs) of the continent and the world. Building on this Brogden presents nine specific proposals that, if adopted, would form the infrastructure of a focused and collaborative church-planting outreach to MUPGs of North Africa by AAGA and AGWM beginning in 2013.

### VIABILITY OF THE RECOMMENDATIONS

The keystone recommendation in Brogden's paper is recommendation 2. All the other proposals flow from this one, and may be adopted in whole or part or significantly revised. Therefore, the focus of this review is on this single key recommendation, which reads, "Let us covenant to be a missionary people who bear God's passion for the whole world, even as we allow Him to lead us to a priority and sequence of focus. Let our first focus be the unengaged Muslim peoples of Mauritania, Morocco, Algeria, Tunisia, Libya, Egypt, Northern Sudan, and Somalia."

The acceptance of this proposal implies two things, that AAGA accepts that it will focus primarily on Muslim unreached people groups and that AAGA accepts a focus on Muslim people that essentially excludes MPUGs in sub-Saharan Africa. Assuming that these assumptions are correct, I offer the following three points of reflection.

## REFLECTION

**Reflection 1: Field Selection**

The fact that Brogden has outlined a basic concrete step forward is positive. In making this recommendation to focus on MUPGs I believe that his proposal may have been further strengthened by explicitly addressing two related questions: (1) Is the Holy Spirit directly impressing or speaking to AAGA about a specific field or fields to enter now (Acts 16:6-9)? (These specific fields may already be among those that he has outlined. There may be no difference, and if so, that is fine.) (2) Are there any doors of opportunity among the MUPG's of North Africa and beyond that are currently open or show clear signs of receptivity? If so, these should be incorporated in the first step.

The primary reason for doing this is to take advantage of the opportunities and thus reap the most accessible harvest within the MUPGs. In addition, in this fledgling stage of coordinated AAGA outreach, it is important to the sustainability of the enterprise that the sending churches be supplied with some stories of success, even if they are scant and the missionaries are overwhelmed by periods of hard work, difficulty, and seemingly no results. While we would like to believe that our national church constituencies are spiritual enough and mature enough to continue to send and support the efforts of their missionaries regardless of results, we must realize that it will take deliberate effort and constant communication to sustain the effort. If in the proposed group of eight church-planting teams there could be at least one that met with a modest degree of evident success (such as some conversions and fellowships established) this would be a great aid in the ongoing communications effort in the sending AAGA churches.

**Reflection 2: Staged Approach**

Allowing for the two year training period, and assuming that Brogden's six stages are adopted in totality and are followed sequentially, this implies that the final deployment of the missionaries in stage six will take place in approximately 2025. Realities on the ground are so dynamic and evolving that it is unlikely that a deployment plan adopted in 2011 this can be followed exactly over the next 14 years. However, rather than ditch the six-stage plan altogether, the AAGA may wish to review the strategy and fields periodically and make firm decisions as to specific fields two years in advance of the time of training sessions for missionaries for those fields.

**Reflection 3: Finances**

The first stage of deployment in 2013 involves the deployment of eight missionary teams from AAGA-related national churches and eight AGWM missionaries. The AAGA missionary couples are each to be fully supported by their respective home churches. While challenging, it is important that this be affirmed as viable by the AAGA churches themselves. It will require increased effort and mobilization within each home church; however, it is an attainable target. It may also be necessary to state explicitly in the main text of the paper that the $2000 per month support is a suggested minimum amount needed, and that some fields may require additional levels of support from the sending church.

In addition, the financial participation of the AAGA-related national churches who do not send a missionary team to North Africa is not clear, particularly during Stage 1 of the plan. Perhaps national churches that do not initially send missionary couples can participate in the raising of the work capital. Although the proposal recommends that AGWM lead the way in raising these funds, this may also be an opportunity for broader participation, even in the early stages of the plan.

# Globalizing Pentecost in Africa: How Can We Proactively Emphasize Pentecost and Mission in Africa and Beyond?

DENZIL R. MILLER

INTRODUCTION

This summit's purpose, as I understand it, is to focus on the role of the Africa Assemblies of God in reaching the unreached of Africa and the nations of the world with the life-changing gospel of Christ before His soon return, and to recommend a way forward for the movement. I have been asked to present this paper on the topic "Globalizing Pentecost in Africa: How Can We Proactively Emphasize Pentecost and Mission in Africa and Beyond?" I begin with some needed definitions:

First, this paper deals with *globalizing* Pentecost and missions in Africa and beyond. The word globalizing, as used in this paper, is not to be confused with the concept of globalization—although globalization will, indeed, impact Africa's participation in missions. Rather, when we speak of globalizing Pentecost and missions, we speak about the focus and target of the emerging missions movement in the Africa Assemblies of God. This focus must include all of Africa and the Indian Ocean Basin, including North Africa. Africa's missionary focus, however, cannot end at the African coastline; it must extend to all the nations of the world, or, in the final words of Jesus, "to the ends of the earth."

In true Pentecostal fashion, Africans must be prepared to go, without restriction, wherever the Spirit directs. History has taught us that when a missionary movement limits its focus to a particular people, place, or area of the world, its vision is often vitiated. Not only are the nations neglected, but the church's effectiveness to the very part of the world on which they are exclusively focusing seems also to be mitigated. From its inception the Assemblies of God has embraced the world as its parish, and it should be no different for our African church. Globalizing Pentecost and missions in Africa and beyond, therefore, speaks of the universalizing of Spirit-empowered, Spirit-directed missions to all people, peoples, and places.

Globalizing thus infers that our missionary emphasis should be on both *all people* and *all peoples,* or, in the words of Jesus, on "every creature" (Mark 16:16) and "every nation" (Matt. 28:19). As the Spirit directs, we must continue to aggressively target receptive individuals and societies wherever they are found. In doing this, however, we must not neglect the hard places. We must proactively, that is, boldly and intentionally, target the remaining unreached people groups of Africa, the Middle East, and beyond. While the African church must think globally, practicality and need will mandate that African missions take a keen interest in the redemptive needs of Africa itself—especially those who have not yet been engaged by a Spirit-empowered missionary movement.

In addition, the idea of globalizing, or universalizing, Pentecost and missions in Africa and beyond can also be applied to the sending base. We thus call on all of the fifty AAGA-related national churches in Africa to proactively take immediate and definite steps to advocate for and experience a nation-wide Pentecostal outpouring in their churches in preparation for aggressive missionary outreach to those who have not yet been effectively engaged with the gospel. One of AAGA's Decade of Pentecost goals is to engage the 806 unreached people groups (according to the Joshua Project) in sub-Sahara Africa by the end of 2020. This will require the proactive participation of every one of our AAGA-related national churches. It will also require creative cooperation between national churches.

God has brought the AG Africa to this moment in history. With 16 million constituents attending 65,000 Assemblies of God churches in Africa and the Indian Ocean Basin, the potential is staggering. We, as God's missionary people, must seize the moment. We must move out quickly in the Spirit's power to proclaim Christ's lordship in all of Africa and beyond.

Further, our challenge is to globalize *Pentecost* and missions in Africa and beyond. Not only must Africa's missionary emphasis be global, but, as indicated above, it must also be authentically Pentecostal. This paper broadly defines the term Pentecost as the complete panoply of biblical understanding, teaching, experience, and approach unique to the Pentecostal church—specifically as it relates to fulfilling the *missio Dei*. The term Pentecost thus speaks of all that it means to be truly Pentecostal as exemplified in the lives and ministries of Jesus and the New Testament disciples.

Biblically understood, the purpose of Pentecost is missions, and the dynamic of missions is Pentecost. Jesus' personal teaching on Pentecost was inherently missional. In His final magisterial promise to His church, He clearly defined the central purpose of Pentecost: "But you will receive power when the Holy Spirit has come upon you, and you will be my witnesses in Jerusalem and in all Judea and Samaria, and to the end of the earth" (Acts 1:8). As Pentecostals, we take Acts as more than sacred history. It is, rather, our present-day, divinely-conceived guide for missions strategy and practice. We thus conceive the book of Acts to be the Spirit's strategic outline for the advancement of God's kingdom—not for the primitive church only, but for the entire church during the entire Age of the Spirit until Jesus comes again.

Finally, we seek to *proactively* emphasize Pentecost and missions in Africa and beyond. During this momentous decade we, as African Pentecostals, choose to not stand with our hands idly folded, passively hoping that a powerful Spirit-empowered, Spirit-directed missions movement will somehow providentially emerge in our Africa Assemblies of God. Rather, we will intentionally and aggressively pursue our God-ordained destiny. Rather than responding retroactively to the spiritual, economic, and societal forces around us, we will proactively pursue the *missio Dei* in the power of the Holy Spirit. With hearts full of anticipation, as the mariner who embarks on a new voyage, we will hoist our sails to the prevailing wind of the Spirit. We will preach and teach pervasively and persuasively on the mission of God. We will aggressively advocate and pray for a powerful new continent-wide Pentecostal outpouring. And we will boldly recruit missionaries and mobilize our churches to send Spirit-empowered missionaries to the unreached people and peoples of Africa and beyond.

## A PROACTIVE MISSIONS MODEL

As we contemplate a model for the emergent missionary movement within the Africa Assemblies of God, which one shall we adopt? Our natural inclination is to accept without question the models that have been lived out before us. While there is much to learn from those with whom we have partnered through the years, we would do well to revisit the mission model of Jesus and the apostles. After all, did not their societal context more closely parallel ours than does the context of our western missionary partners? Those first-century missionaries emerged from societies that had been colonized, marginalized, and impoverished. And yet, because they rightly perceived themselves to be divinely called and commissioned, and because they unquestioningly and enthusiastically obeyed Christ's command to be empowered by the Spirit, they changed the very course of human history.

I propose that the ministries of Jesus and the apostles as portrayed in the gospels and Acts become Africa's guiding missionary model. I recommend that we prayerfully and contemplatively peer again into Scripture, especially the Acts of the Apostles, to find a truly Pentecostal model for our missions endeavors. What then do we mean when we say that we should proactively adopt a Pentecostal missions model in Africa and beyond? As I envision it, such a missions model must include at least four essential components:

### A Pentecostal Understanding of Mission

First, our missions model must include a uniquely Pentecostal understanding of missions. This means that we must proactively develop and widely propagate a truly Pentecostal understanding of missions in an African context. In doing this, we must formulate a comprehensive understanding of the role of the Holy Spirit in missional ministry. In my considered opinion, such a well-conceived, broad-based, and contextualized Pentecostal understanding of missions is largely absent in our Assemblies of God churches across Africa. Generally speaking, we have not done as well as we could have in articulating and living out such a truly Pentecostal understanding of missions. Thankfully, this lack of understanding has been addressed through conferences, such as Eleventh Hour Institutes, Acts 1:8 Conferences, and Schools of the Spirit conducted across the continent. It has further been addressed in the development of missional textbooks, such as *The Biblical Theology of Missions*,[1] *A History of the Church in Africa: A Survey from a Pentecostal Perspective*,[2] and others, produced by the Africa's Hope Discovery Series. These efforts, however, must be viewed as just a beginning. Much remains to be done. Here, at the beginning of this Decade of Pentecost, a scholarly study investigating the level of truly missional and Pentecostal understanding in the Africa Assemblies of God would indeed be useful. I, therefore, call on our emerging African scholars to step up and address this issue from a clearly African perspective.

A truly Pentecostal missiology should include, not only a Pentecostal understanding of missions, but a missional understanding of Pentecost. This understanding should clearly answer such questions as, "How does our understanding of, and experience with, the Spirit impact the way we do missions? How does it affect the way we proclaim Christ to the lost? How does it impact the way contextualize the message? How does our experience with the Spirit shape the way we respond to human need? How should our uniquely Pentecostal understanding of missions influence the way we plant indigenous missionary churches? How should it impact the way we penetrate new fields? Or the way we engage unreached (and sometimes hostile) people groups? How does our understanding of, and experience with, the Spirit inform the way we develop effective missionary strategies? Or the way we mobilize the laity for missions? Or the way we raise the necessary assets to fund the mission?" Our experience with the Spirit should dramatically impact the way we approach all of these missional issues, as well as other unnamed issues. A clear and comprehensive Pentecostal theology of missionary praxis is needed if we are to effectively globalize Pentecost and missions in Africa and beyond during this providential decade.

## A Spirit-empowered Missionary Force

Secondly, a truly proactive model of Pentecostal missions means that we single-mindedly pursue a Spirit-empowered missionary force. In doing this, we must ensure that every missionary we receive, recruit, and deploy is truly a man or woman of the Spirit. This means that they must have been truly and powerfully baptized in the Spirit resulting in both Spirit-inspired tongues and Spirit-empowered witness (Acts 2:4; 1:8). Further, we must ensure that these "Pentecostal apostles" are people sensitive to the voice of the Spirit and able to walk in close step with the Spirit (Gal. 5:25 NIV). They must be people of much prayer with lives and ministries evidencing both the gifts and fruit of the Spirit. All other personal, academic, or professional qualifications, while important, must be viewed as secondary. The lives and ministries of these genuinely Pentecostal missionaries must clearly demonstrate passion for lost and compassion for the suffering. They must be adept at leading sinners to Christ and believers into the baptism in the Holy Spirit. They must further be able to effectively disciple these same believers and lead them into Spirit-empowered missional ministry. Finally, this new breed of African missionaries must clearly understand that the disciples they make, and churches they plant, must be empowered by the Holy Spirit and wholly committed to Christ and His mission. This assessment applies both to the missionaries *sent out* by our African churches and to the missionaries *received* by the church in Africa. If we are to truly globalize Pentecost and missions in Africa, we must insist that every missionary, from and to Africa, be a man or woman of the Spirit.

**A Pentecostal Strategy**

Thirdly, a truly proactive Pentecostal model of missions means that we intentionally develop and aggressively implement a genuinely Pentecostal missions strategy. As mentioned above, our unique Pentecostal experience and understanding of ministry must be brought to bear in developing such a strategy of missions. Historically, Pentecostal missiologists have prayerfully probed the book of Acts to find their missionary strategy. They have approached the book as a living paradigm of evangelistic and missionary practice. In doing so, they have noted that in Acts the Holy Spirit is presented as the executive of the missionary enterprise. From beginning to end He is portrayed as the Superintendent of the Harvest, that is, the one who fills, empowers, inspires, anoints, directs, sends, guides, enlightens, and encourages the missionary enterprise.

In recent years we have observed the term "strategy of the Spirit" used in various ways and in various contexts by missionary strategists.[3] In the gospels and Acts we are presented with, what I believe to be, a true strategy of the Spirit. It is a strategy employed by both Jesus and the apostles. This missionary strategy is notably evident in the missionary ministry of Paul as presented in the book of Acts—especially during his Ephesian campaign (19:1-11)—and described in his epistles (most clearly in Romans 15:14-20). A close examination of Paul's missionary strategy reveals that he was merely emulating the strategy of God the Father in sending Jesus into the world, and the strategy of Jesus in sending His church into the world. This strategy includes certain key elements, including the necessity of the "sent ones" being empowered by the Spirit, a clear Spirit-anointed proclamation of the gospel accompanied by confirmatory signs and wonders, and the intentional planting of Spirit-empowered missionary churches. This New Testament strategy of the Spirit further includes the mobilizing of Spirit-empowered missionary churches through formal training, informal mentoring, and sending.

In preparation for his visit to Rome, Paul outlined his missionary strategy (Rom. 15:14-21). This outline can serve as a pattern for Pentecostal missionary ministry today. Here Paul described his missionary ministry as being Christ-centered (vv. 17-19), Spirit-empowered (v. 19), divinely-authenticated by signs and wonders (v. 19), proclamationally-oriented (v. 20), and apostolically-functioning, that is, steadfastly focused on "those who have never heard" the gospel (vv. 20-21). If we are to effectively globalize Pentecost and missions in Africa and beyond, our missionary strategies must proactively include each of the above-mentioned elements.

## A Spirit-empowered Church

Finally, our missions model must include a commitment to *intentionally* plant thousands of avant-garde, Spirit-empowered missionary churches throughout Africa, and wherever else we may go. Jesus himself intentionally and proactively planted a Spirit-empowered missionary church (Luke 24:46-49; Acts 1:4-8) as did the apostles after Him (Acts 2:38-39; 8:14-18; 9:1-7; Rom.15:17-20; 1 Cor. 2:1-5; 1 Thess. 1:5-8). Because they expected every disciple to be a witness, they expected every disciple to be empowered by the Spirit. We must expect the same today, and we must intentionally work to see our churches universally empowered by the Spirit and unwaveringly focused on the *missio Dei*.

## TOWARD A WORKABLE STRATEGY: HOW CAN WE EFFECTIVELY GLOBALIZE PENTECOST AND MISSIONS IN AFRICA AND BEYOND?

If we sincerely desire to globalize Pentecost and missions in Africa and beyond, what is the way forward? What plan of action shall we adopt? I suggest that our action plan comprise at least five key elements. It must be (1) solidly biblical, (2) intentionally missional, (3) authentically Pentecostal, (4) boldly proactive, and (5) thoroughly comprehensive. Let us examine each of these elements.

**Solidly Biblical**

The first element of our plan to globalize Pentecost and missions in Africa and beyond is scriptural fidelity. We as Assemblies of God believers view the Bible as God's divinely-inspired revelation to humankind. It is our sole and final authority for doctrine and practice. We are unapologetically a "people of the Book." Therefore, any plan to globalize Pentecost and missions in Africa and beyond must, above all else, be based solidly on the teachings of Scripture. The first question, then, that we must ask is, "What does the Bible have to say on the subject?" Our challenge is to be relevant to the ever-changing and multifaceted contexts in Africa, while, at the same time, remaining faithful to God's word.

Therefore, as we strategize to globalize Pentecost and missions in the Africa Assemblies of God, we must embrace the Bible as our strategic handbook. The story of the early church as depicted in the book of Acts is especially relevant. It is our only divinely-inspired record of how the early church carried out Christ's directive to take the gospel to the nations. Our Pentecostal forefathers found great inspiration and insight in its pages, embracing it as their master plan for normative experience and practice. The strategies they gleaned from the book of Acts helped to catapult the Pentecostal church into worldwide prominence, enabling it to outstrip all other religious movements in expansion and church growth, particularly in the Global South. Amazingly, in just over a century there now exists more than one million local Pentecostal churches around the world.

As a movement we must, once again, take up the book of Acts, not merely to read it as a historical record of the ancient beginnings of the church, but to pour over its pages in search for missions strategy. Acts teaches us that the biblical answer to a waning of missionary zeal in the church is recurrent and pervasive outpourings of the Spirit. It further teaches that these outpourings must occur in an overtly missional context. These cardinal understandings must become integral components of our plan of advance.

**Intentionally Missional**

A second element of our plan to globalize Pentecost and missions in Africa and beyond is intentionality. That is, we must be intentionally missional in all that we do. As Pentecostals, we are not only a people of the Book, we are also a people on mission. We conceive ourselves to be an integral segment of God's last-days missionary people. In recent years this fact has gripped the African church as never before. Across the continent Assemblies of God churches have begun to re-envision and reinvent themselves. They have become increasing missional in their posture and practice.

Beginning with the Decade of Harvest of the 1990s, and continuing to the present, our Africa Assemblies of God churches have begun to re-envision themselves as vital players in God's last-days missionary enterprise. They have begun to see themselves, not so much as a impoverished people gathered for personal blessing, but as an empowered people scattered in missional witness. No longer do they conceive themselves to be merely those who receive missionary assistance from abroad; they have begun to re-envision themselves as an indispensable part of God's missionary-sending people. And yet, while all of this is true, in many of our churches across the continent, both national and local, the process has only begun. We must, therefore, wholeheartedly commit ourselves to broadly and proactively encouraging this Spirit-inspired process.

In addition to re-envisioning themselves as full participants in the *missio Dei*, our Africa Assemblies of God churches have begun the arduous, yet essential, process of reinventing themselves. The path leading from western dependency to true missional indigeniety is long, rugged, and fraught with dangers. The journey requires the wisdom and perseverance that only the Spirit can give. Nevertheless, across the continent our Assemblies of God churches have confidently begun the journey. While they are at differing points along the way, the good news is that most, if not all, have at least begun the journey. We are believing God that, during this Decade of Pentecost, a true missional transformation will occur, not only within the African church, but also in its missionary partners from around the world. With the new challenges of the twenty-first century looming, the unreached people and peoples of Africa and the world beckoning, and the missionary Spirit of God directing, we must deliberately and boldly reinvent ourselves. New and more dynamic—that is, more authentically missional—paradigms of partnership must emerge as, together, we seek the wisdom and direction of the Lord.

**Authentically Pentecostal**

A third necessary component of our plan to globalize Pentecost and missions in Africa and beyond is a clear understanding of what it means to be authentically Pentecostal. In other words, if we seek to globalize Pentecost in Africa, we must be certain that the Pentecost we are globalizing is authentic. That is, it must be the "real thing" as believed upon, experienced, and lived out by Jesus, the apostles, and the first-century believers.

Therefore, in determining our way forward we will not raise our finger to the sky to test the ever-changing winds of doctrine or practice that all-to-often blow through the Pentecostal/charismatic movement. Neither will our way forward be determined in the fickled courts of public opinion, or by the latest church growth theory or leadership trend. Nor will we be driven by the ever-shifting waves of donor preference, no matter how tempting or generous their offers may seem. Rather, our eyes will remain fixed on the mandates of Scripture and our ears will stay attuned to the voice of the Spirit. We will faithfully seek to discern His will and His way.

Rather than asking, "What is the anticipated logical outcome of our strategic decisions?" we will first ask, "What is the source, or origin, of this strategy? From whence does it come? Does it rise out human reason or out of the Spirit's impulse?"[4] As authentically Pentecostal missionaries, our strategic decisions must not be intellect-driven, emotion-driven, or donor-driven; they must, rather, above all else, be biblically informed and Spirit-driven. In other words, our focus must be on a biblically-sound, missional exegesis of Scripture, accompanied by a clearly-discerned voice of the Spirit.

## Boldly Proactive

A fourth element that we must incorporate into our plan to globalize Pentecost and missions in Africa and beyond is proactivity. That is, we must assume a posture that is boldly proactive. If we are to lead our churches into powerful Pentecostal and missional renewal, we must regard the issue as our top priority. We cannot view it as one among other equally-important agenda items. It must become, and remain, "job number one" for the church. The issue of authentic Pentecostal revival is of such significance that it demands our primary and sustained attention. The quest for the Spirit's empowering presence must be placed and remain at center stage in the church's planning and activities.

Jesus himself placed the empowering of the church at center stage. To Him it was not a side issue to be tabled and taken up at next quarter's business meeting. In His mind it was of supreme importance, demanding the church's immediate and focused attention (Luke 24:29; Acts 1:4-8). We, too, must be gripped by this fact: if the Africa Assemblies of God is to become the missions force God intends for it to be, we must have widespread and recurring Pentecostal revival. And this revival must occur in a thoroughly missional context. All other issues must become, and remain, secondary.

This missional revival can only be accomplished through a determined and energetic pursuit of authentic Pentecostal power. We must, therefore, pursue every means possible to actively encourage individual and group initiative across the continent. Further, we must persevere in our pursuit of Pentecostal renewal until the desired outcomes are achieved—a Spirit-empowered, missionally-focused church actively engaged in reaching the unreached with the good news of Christ.

## Purposefully Comprehensive

A fifth component of our plan to globalize Pentecost and missions in Africa and beyond is comprehensiveness. If we are to see a powerful Spirit-empowered missionary movement rise out of the Africa Assemblies of God, our strategy for bringing Pentecostal and missional renewal to the continent must be all-encompassing. In other words, it must target every facet of Assemblies of God church life. Not only must the issue of Pentecostal revival target every person in the church, it must be addressed in every available forum, utilize every necessary means, and be applied at all possible times. This comprehensive approach must include the following:

*1. Every person.* When calling our churches to Pentecostal and missional renewal, effort must be made to ensure that every person and every grouping of people in the church is adequately targeted. This includes national, district, sectional, and local church leadership. It also includes departmental leadership, such as Sunday school, men's, women's, youth, university, humanitarian, and children's ministry leaders. Institutional leadership must not be neglected. Bible school administration and teachers must be targeted, since these individuals are often the key influencers in the church. In targeting every person, care must also be taken to include diverse language groups and differing economic and social strata. Our effort to globalize Pentecost and missions in the Africa Assemblies of God must reach to every member and attender in the church.

*2. Every forum.* In designing a comprehensive response to the need to bring authentic Pentecostalism to the church in Africa, every forum and delivery system must be employed. The general assemblies and special gatherings of the church must be utilized, including general councils, district councils, sectional councils, local church services, home cell gatherings, school chapels, spiritual emphases, and more.

Print and broadcast media must also be put to use and distributed widely. Print media could include books, tracts, flyers, magazines, Bible studies, and sermon outlines. New lessons and study guides could be purchased or produced for Sunday school and home cell study. Broadcast media, including radio, television, and the Internet should also be used.

*3. Every means.* The church must use every means at its disposal to address the need for Pentecostal and missional renewal. In addition to those mentioned above, these means could include preaching, teaching, writing, seminars, revival meetings, and specially-called conferences and assemblies.

*4. All times.* A comprehensive response to globlizing Pentecost and missions in our churches cannot be limited to a single event or even a series of special events. One gathering, or even a series of gatherings (such as an Eleventh Hour Institute or an Acts 1:8 Conference—as significant as these events can be), will not get the job done. That is why AAGA's ten-year Decade of

Pentecost emphasis is called for, where the church throws the full weight of its influence and resources behind these most pressing of all needs.

## DECADE OF PENTECOST AS METANARRATIVE

In March of 2009, at the quadrennial meeting of the General Assembly of the Africa Assemblies of God Alliance in Honeydew, South Africa, the assembled delegates from across Africa unanimously adopted a resolution declaring 2010-2020 as a "Decade of Pentecost" in the Africa Assemblies of God (see Appendix 1). In the resolution AAGA called on its "constituent national churches to promote a Pentecostal awakening in their churches aimed at empowering the church for greater evangelistic, missionary, and church-planting involvement." The resolution further stated that "the Assemblies of God in Africa set as its goal to see 10 million of our members baptized in the Holy Spirit" during the ten years from 2010 to 2020. Since that time, other goals have been advanced, including the following:

- Marshaling 10 million new Spirit-empowered witnesses who will actively share the gospel with their friends and neighbors.
- Aggressively planting tens of thousands of new Spirit-empowered missionary churches across the continent.
- Mobilizing 100,000 intercessors who will pray daily for a powerful Pentecostal outpouring on the African church.
- Recruiting, training, and deploying hundreds of cross-cultural missionaries to Africa and beyond.
- Engaging the 800+ yet-to-be-reached-tribes of sub-Sahara Africa.

The Decade of Pentecost was officially launched across Africa on the Day of Pentecost, March 23, 2010. Most of our AAGA-related national churches across Africa have officially joined the Decade of Pentecost emphasis, setting aggressive evangelistic, church planting, missionary, and renewal goals. These national churches have begun to actively mobilize themselves to achieve these faith-filled goals. This Decade of Pentecost emphasis holds the potential of becoming the most fruitful evangelistic and missionary thrust in the 100-year history of the Assemblies of God in Africa, even surpassing the now historic Decade of Harvest emphasis of the 1990s.

I, therefore, propose that the Africa Assemblies of God World Missions Commission enthusiastically embrace and aggressively promote this AAGA initiative as its primary method of globalizing Pentecost and missions in Africa and beyond. I do this for three reasons:

### The Decade of Pentecost as Mobilization

True Pentecostal revival is about empowering the church to complete the Great Commission of Christ (Acts 1:8). As previously stated, if the Africa Assemblies of God is to maximize its effectiveness in mobilizing itself to send missionaries to the nations, proclaiming the gospel to the lost, overcoming and defeating demonic opposition to the gospel, planting Spirit-empowered missional churches, showing Christ's compassion to the hurting, and reaching the unreached peoples of Africa and beyond, the movement must experience a continent-wide Pentecostal outpouring with millions of its members being baptized in the Holy Spirit and empowered for the task at hand. Further, as noted, this continent-wide outpouring must be experienced in an overtly missional context as is was in the early church. AAGA's Decade of Pentecost emphasis provides an efficient framework for this to occur. As more and more leaders, pastors, churches, and missionaries across Africa embrace the initiative, it will gain even greater momentum. Further, the Decade of Pentecost emphasis has huge promotional potential. It is a theme which we can all rally around, both in Africa and in America, to help create missional awareness and raise the necessary prayer and financial support needed to move quickly forward.

### The Decade of Pentecost as Alignment

Leadership practitioners understand that for an organization to achieve maximum effectiveness it must achieve what is known as "organizational alignment." This means that every department and person in the organization must be unified and moving in the same direction, seeking to fulfill the same clearly-defined goals. If we are to effectively globalize Pentecost and missions in Africa and beyond, continental alignment is essential.

And yet, we must come to terms with the daunting fact that mobilizing and unifying a movement as massive and diverse as the Assemblies of God in Africa is an almost impossible endeavor. Thus the question, "How do we go about unifying 16 million constituents from hundreds of language, ethnic, and cultural backgrounds attending 65,000 local churches affiliated with 50 national churches across sub-Sahara Africa and the Indian Ocean basin?" Add to these potentially fragmenting dynamics the fact that these churches, and the missionary organizations they work with, are already actively engaged in a multitude of potentially competing and conflicting programs and initiatives. Further, how can we facilitate unified action between missionary sending agencies and missionary receiving churches; between missionaries with their own agendas and national churches with sometimes contravening agendas? How can we foster unified action between various national churches in neighboring countries—and sometimes even between national churches within the borders of a single country? How can we unify the visions of national church leaders with those of local pastors and churches? How can we unify the various training, humanitarian, evangelistic, and missionary initiatives across the continent, each with their own goals and emphases? How can we bring new and emerging churches and ministries into alignment with what is already happening in existing churches and ministries? These and a multitude of other factors mitigate against unity in the Africa Assemblies of God and its partnering organizations. How then do we bring Pentecostal and missional alignment to the Assemblies of God in Africa?

I suggest that AAGA's Decade of Pentecost initiative can serve as the grand metanarrative, or unifying theme, for the Africa Assemblies of God and its missionary partners. If universally embraced and encouraged, the continental emphasis can become a powerful aligning force in the Assemblies of God in Africa for the next ten years and beyond. Its theme is broad enough in scope to include everyone and every organizational entity in our churches, yet narrow enough to keep us all moving in the same direction, that is, the fulfillment of the *missio Dei* in the power of the Holy Spirit.

**The Decade of Pentecost as Corrective**

The Decade of Pentecost emphasis can serve the Africa Assemblies of God in yet another crucial way, that is, as a corrective. Like a ship that has lost its rudder, much of Africa's Pentecostalism has drifted frighteningly off course. In many cases it has forfeited its missionary soul, becoming self-centered and self-engrossed. Tragically, in far too many instances, this departure from the way includes some of our own Assemblies of God churches. Many have been swept away by the prosperity mania that has engulfed much of the continent. While we believe in and advocate a truly biblical prosperity, one aimed at equipping and enabling the church to fulfill its missionary mandate, the quasi-biblical, hyper-prosperity advocated by many must be challenged and corrected. If Pentecostalism in Africa does not recapture its missionary soul, it is in grave danger of becoming sidelined as God's agency for evangelizing the nations before Christ's soon coming. The Decade of Pentecost is a ready vehicle that can serve to remind us of who we are: we are God's last-days, Spirit-empowered missionary people.

## CONCLUSION

As we contemplate Africa's missionary future, and our part in that future, we must come to terms with what it means to be truly Pentecostal and truly Assemblies of God. And, as we seek to more clearly understand and more pervasively disseminate to our churches the concepts of what it means to be authentically Pentecostal, we must prayerfully address two critical issues:

First, *we must learn to do Pentecost missionally,* that is, we must "missionize" our Pentecostalism. We must abandon the self-serving, inwardly-focused hybrid of Pentecostalism that has overtaken much of the continent, and we must, once again, enthusiastically embrace the mission of Jesus and joyously respond to His final mandate of Acts 1:8.

Not only must we learn to do Pentecost missionally, *we must learn to do missions Pentecostally.* In other words, we must "Pentecostalize" our missions. As we seek to fulfill Christ's command to take the gospel to the unreached of Africa and the nations, we must never forget that God has freely given to us His Spirit to enable us to accomplish this task. We must be ever conscious that the Spirit of the Lord is upon us, as He was upon Jesus, to anoint us to proclaim the gospel to the poor, to heal the brokenhearted, and to proclaim deliverance to the captives. Never again can we relegate our Pentecostal experience and understanding to the church building. We must take it to the streets and ultimately to the nations. Whatever we do, whether preaching the gospel, planting new churches, penetrating new fields, showing compassion to the hurting, training pastors, or anything else we do, we must do it all in the Spirit's power. May the Lord of the Harvest empower us and guide us as we seek to globalize Pentecost and missions in Africa and beyond.

---

ENDNOTES

[1] Paul B. York, Springfield, MO: Life Publishers International, 2008.

[2] Jerry Spain, Springfield, Life Publishers International, 2009.

[3] I myself expand on the term in *Empowered for Global Mission: A Missionary Look at the Book of Acts* (Springfield, MO: Life Publishers, 2008), 240-248, and in *Implications of Lukan Pneumatology: A Doctoral Study Guide,* 3rd ed. (Lome, Togo: Pan Africa Theological Seminary, 2009), 55-56.

[4] I first discovered this concept in the writings of the late Anglican missiologist, Roland Allen.

# Globalizing Pentecost in Africa: A Response to the Paper by Denzil R. Miller

LAZARUS CHAKWERA

Dr. Denzil R. Miller has truly grasped what it would take to "globalize Pentecost and missions" in the Africa Assemblies of God. If leaders at every level and believers in the Africa Assemblies of God would catch this vision, feel the burden, and do their part, the world could literally "turn upside down."

The emphasis is well placed that "a truly Pentecostal understanding of missions should include, not only a Pentecostal understanding of missions, but a missional understanding of Pentecost." This can indeed help align the movement into one agenda, that is, the *missio Dei*. Many times and in many quarters, the power of Pentecost is sought and valued only for personal gain. The power of God is perceived as being for personal breakthroughs—an anointing for the raising of the Christian from a lowly life to a prosperous, healthy, and happy life. The power of the Spirit becomes primarily the answer to the African problem of pain, poverty, misery and disease. Miller is right that a clear emphasis on the missional objective of Pentecost can help in setting our priority.

The challenge is laid out as Miller writes, "In true Pentecostal fashion, Africans must be prepared to go, without restriction, wherever the Spirit directs." There is no doubt or question that the Spirit as superintendent of the work of harvest intends to send Africans literally to the entire world. The doubt or question arises when one starts thinking about whether the African church is ready to be sent, whether the African church is alert enough to be preparing for such an awesome "unfinished task."

More doubts can arise as we deem ourselves unable to "compete" with the missions model of Western missionaries. Maybe our sending base cannot be as structured and as wealthy as the western missionary sending agencies. Maybe it would take generations to establish the sending mentality within the 50 national churches and the 16 million strong church meeting in 65,000 local gatherings. This is where I find Miller's suggestion, that we take the missions model of Jesus and the apostles, very hopeful. Africa can arise just like the early church because the social political-economic circumstances troubling the early church did not stop that Pentecostal community from carrying out their mandate to the whole world.

For instance, the Spirit can use the Diaspora of Africans, which comes as a result of various political, socio-economical reasons to reach the world just like the early church was scattered by persecution and yet carried out the mission of God. We may not be prepared to do missions if we fail to recognize such unconventional "means" of doing or sending missionaries. It is not missions only when a sending agency can facilitate financial support for the missionary, but it is missions even when the missionary supports himself as did Paul in his "tentmaking" business.

The "game changer" for Jesus and the apostles was not their status, money, acumen, or any other earthly factor. It was the endowment with power from on high that brought world changing results. The same Spirit can fill us and do a mighty work in the earth that cannot be explained in terms of money or human effort.

But can the diverse African Assemblies of God unify themselves and pull together the net? A generation filled with the Holy Spirit brings with it a sense of urgency to organize and send. A great authentic outpouring of the Spirit can truly help align all of the AG national churches for this great mission. Miller's proposal makes sense when he recommends "that the Africa Assemblies of God World Missions Commission embrace and aggressively promote this AAGA initiative [Decade of Pentecost] as its primary method of globalizing Pentecost and missions in Africa and beyond." His observation is significant that, "as a unifying and aligning theme, it is broad enough in scope to include everyone and every organizational entity in our churches, yet narrow enough to keep us all moving in the same direction, that is, the fulfillment of the *missio Dei* in the power of the Spirit."

Perhaps more discussion is needed now to illuminate how the coming of the Spirit, as we seek Him in the Decade of Pentecost, helps fulfill the Great Commission of Christ, not in just the proclamation of the gospel, but in making disciples. We know that discipling is an integral part of the mandate of Christ. The Pentecostal experience, then, ought to help in the process of, not just conversion, but in establishing discipleship. In other words, there is a didactic and discipleship purpose of Pentecost. Considering the influx of heresy and cults within Christendom, and false religions without, how does Pentecost solve the problem of shallow Christianity in Africa? After all, Paul was led by the Spirit to go back to the places where he had established churches to see the progress. What is the role of the Spirit in preserving the harvest? Is the Decade of Pentecost also a season for such truth encounters? Is truth encounter within the boundaries of our most strict understanding of the *missio Dei*?

Another area that needs more emphasis is the area of power encounter. The need for the Spirit is probably more acute for the African believer because of the pervasive animist and superstitious context. The African believer, then, can easily appreciate the value of the Pentecostal experience if the *missio Dei* is understood in spiritual warfare terms. This empowering is also for battle to rescue and deliver a lost people. It is not simply the boldness to open one's mouth and proclaim or witness Christ to one's neighbor but power to handle and subdue all the power of the evil one, to bind the strong man and plunder his possessions. To a certain extent, then, Pentecost is to be perceived as personal "power supply" in the daily battle against the enemy of our souls. Of course, a line has to be drawn between this and the selfish "breakthrough source" that many have construed the Spirit's purpose to be.

And finally, the outpouring of the Holy Spirit cannot be understood to apply to AAGA alone. God said that He would pour out His Spirit upon everyone regardless of their societal standing. How does AAGA relate with others who are equally Spirit-filled and missional in orientation in order to finish the Great Commission together? This might help us see ourselves as part of a wider body of Christ and, therefore, see our role as that which compliments rather than competes. May the Decade of Pentecost and the World Missions Commission of AAGA spearhead a catalytic movement that helps flood the earth with the knowledge of the Lord as the waters cover the sea!

*Globalizing Pentecost in Africa: A Response*

# Missional Mentoring: How National Churches with Strong and Effective Missions Outreaches Can Mentor Those Without

ANTONIO PEDROZO AND BRAD WALZ

THE GREAT MISSIONS POTENTIAL WITHIN OUR STRONG NATIONAL CHURCHES IN AFRICA AND THE WORLD

**People Potential**

The western churches of the World Assemblies of God represents about 7 to 10% of our worldwide constituency. With a current missions force of more than 4,500, including short term (1-2 year) workers, if we would reach that level of proportional effort worldwide, we would have more than 45,000 workers. That is more than ten times our present number. That is an enormous people potential.

**Economic Potential**

If every non-western believer in our worldwide AG fellowship gave just one US dollar per month to world missions (an amount that is very reachable in 90% of the countries), missions funds would be available in excess of $720,000,000 per month. That is triple the present giving of the US Assemblies of God. Many nations who consider themselves too poor to do missions, when taking a basic product such as bread, rice, or beans and applying the value of a small amount (such as a kilo or a one-time serving) are shocked to discover the potential. If everyone in their national church gave such a minimal amount per month, their missions giving would be in the hundreds of thousands, or even millions, of dollars. The economic potential is staggering.

**Spiritual Potential**

The possibilities of younger churches that have been more recently birthed in revival joining us in the worldwide fields adds tremendous spiritual potential to the movement. Non-western dynamics such as spiritual warfare, cross-cultural sensitivity, sacrifice, faith, and belief in miracles could bring new vitality and balance to our western perspective. Consider, as well, the area of prayer. To have 60,000,000 believers worldwide praying for the three great resistant religious blocks (Islamic, Hindu, and Buddhist) could bring new energy to intercession and prayer movements.

**Cultural Potential**

Westerners are often shunned by people belonging to the world's three great resistant religious blocks. These people are very suspicious that westerners will try to impose their cultural mores on them. Although there are notable exceptions, missionaries with non-western passports and varying skin tones are not as likely to encounter the same resistance. The "gap principal" applies here. Since there is less of an economic and cultural distance between many non-western missionaries and the unreached peoples they are targeting than there is with western missionaries, these Two-thirds World missionaries have less of a "comfort and convenience gap" to bridge. This can often translate into quicker adjustment on the field, which can then result in quicker acceptance on the part of nationals. Obviously, Two-thirds World missionaries will also experience culture shock and adjustments; however, there remains a great potential for more effective missions work in many contexts. This can result in the multiplication of our worldwide efforts. Our present challenge is, then, how to make this strategy become a reality.

Antonio Pedrozo and Brad Walz

## THE REALITY OF OUR SITUATION: A LACK OF "SERIOUS SENDERS."

Missiologists agree on the need of reaching the "least reached" peoples of the world with the gospel. And it is obvious that if more countries are involved in mobilizing and deploying workers, the task will be more effectively engaged. Our challenge, however, is how to make this happen in a realistic way. Before we consider how national churches with strong missionary programs can help mentor those with emerging missions programs, let us consider the reality of what is happening in our world, particularly in Africa.

Missiologists have often touted how the "Global South" (or the non-traditional senders) has surpassed the traditional-sending West in the number of missionaries deployed. Rob Moll's article, "Missions Incredible," found in the March 1, 2006, issue of *Christianity Today,* is one example of such observations:

> ...mission scholars agree that Koreans are a potent vanguard for an emerging missionary movement that is about to eclipse centuries of Western-dominated Protestant missions. They call it the "majority-world" mission movement. They say this new term—"majority world"—is necessary to replace the aging terms "third world" and "developing world." The radical change in Protestant missions is forcing scholars and missionaries to create new ways of talking about the global scene.

However, in our opinion, as we have stated in papers presented to the Missions Commission of the World Assemblies of God Fellowship (WAGF), those assumptions are doubtful, and, at best, have no hard data to back them up. Brad Walz, in a paper for the International Journal of Pentecostal Missions, makes the following observations:

> Let me start with Latin America. Consider the fact that the Latin churches are some of the strongest within the WAGF, and, as a bloc, possibly the strongest in the world. In every Spanish-speaking country, with maybe one exception, the Assemblies of God are a strong force within that nation's evangelical community, and, in most cases, would be considered the largest evangelical body within that nation. Yet from these twenty Spanish-speaking countries there are less than 500 documented

missionaries sent out to other countries. These missionaries are from twenty of the larger, stronger, Assemblies of God national churches in the world! If you remove the three largest senders, that number is reduced to just over 200 workers.

One of our very large AG churches in Latin America (though there is no doubt that it is sending out many missionaries) lacks a central office that would be able to provide reliable statistics. In a private conversation with the then leader of the church, he stated that they knew of 2,000 missionaries being sent out by the church to 17 nations. Surprisingly, 250 of those missionaries were documented as having been sent to Argentina. The vast majority of those 250, however, would not be missionaries as we define them, but rather lay workers living and working in a neighboring country. At this time it would be impossible to produce a realistic statistic, but surely the number of 2,000 does not reflect the number of missionaries actual being sent and supported by the church as cross-cultural workers.

One Asian country has talked about sending out 850 workers. However, in a private conversation with one of their leaders in 2009, he acknowledged to me that "most of that number are pastors who have gone to other countries and are pastoring churches of our language and culture. They are not cross-cultural workers. We possibly have 110 supported cross-cultural workers."

The lack of hard data makes it difficult to make an accurate appraisal. However, in 2007-2008 our committee secretary did such a survey. After receiving responses from national churches from around the world we came up with a "Report on Sending by the National Churches of the WAGF," dated August 2008. Here is what we discovered:

- Number of missionaries sent out by European and North American traditional sending nations:   4,264
- Number of missionaries sent out by "new senders" in the Global South:   1,073
- Undocumented workers (i.e., general numbers without a data base) sent out from the Global South:   4,481
- Total missionaries sent:   9,824

If you include undocumented workers, the new senders have surpassed the traditional ones. However, many of those undocumented workers are short term, or they are not working among another culture/language groups. In other cases a local church has counted every emigrant that has relocated to another country for secular work as a "missionary." The problem with this scenario is that, if there is no database with missionaries' names and addresses, anyone can throw out any number. This kind of thing does not help the cause of world evangelization.

A colleague of mine observed a key problem faced in developing strong missions programs in national churches of the Global South: "Our Latin network has been functioning formally since 1998, and informally going back to the late 80's. We have hard data for the statistics of the Spanish-speaking part. For example, in 2009, $4,203,973.13 was given through the missions departments of those 20 nations. But the two greatest obstacles we have found in having effective and strong sending structures has been that of having the right and experienced leadership, and confronting a poverty mentality which still strangles so many churches."

The poverty mentality remains a serious challenge. There was, and is, significant resistance to missions vision by many pastors who view missions as a threat. It is seen as something that will take funds away from their local churches and from the assets they need to expand their ministries and vision for their local communities. If this is a problem in nations where strong missions structures and support systems have existed for more than twenty years, how much more might it be a reality in regions where missions is just getting started?

The Latin America AG has had a ten- to twenty-year history of missions formation, teaching, networking, and events. And yet the poverty mentality remains formidable. In one national church, one of the strongest in the world, giving for foreign missions averages just 44 cents per church per month. Not per person, per church. This is a sad reality in many of our national churches around the world. If this is true of a Latin church, which has been challenged both denominationally and interdenominationally for more than twenty years, what is the reality in Africa, Eastern Europe, and even parts of Asia where, in most cases, fewer years have been spent in challenging the church that "we can do this too!"

This being said, the bigger problem we face is not having the right leadership. In country after country, not having the right leader has been an impediment to a structure which many young people and missions-minded pastors yearn for. The great challenge in a church with no missions experience is to have leadership that can guide them towards having their first missions experiences. Across the world, in country after country, the right leadership would speed up the process and growth required for an effective missions sending structure.

There is little doubt as to the great potential of the church in the Global South to impact the nations. This is particularly true among the neediest and the least-reached peoples of the world. But, once again, the challenge is how to get from where we are now to where God wants us to be. Before we consider how stronger countries can help the weaker or newer ones, let us first discuss the characteristics of a mature missions department.

## CHARACTERISTICS OF A MATURE MISSIONS DEPARTMENT

Two important missional principles apply here. The first is that everything that is worth something, takes time. You cannot mature instantly. On your way to missional maturity, you will make mistakes, confront and win battles, and have experiences impossible to get from books or theory. The second principle is that in order to achieve maturity a missions department must have the right leader. Many times, a country is ripe for blessing, but the right leader has not been formed, or is not willing serve, or has not been selected to take on the challenge. As well, a real challenge for most of our sending-South nations is that they do not have a missions leader with missionary experience. Therefore, they are limited as to how far they can take the department.

However, after about ten years missionaries will have returned from the field who can help and eventually become leaders. Most of our missions efforts in the sending South, however, are in the pioneer stage, and have few or no sent missionaries with real-life experience. The challenge then becomes how to continue on the next level of maturity.

## A Mature Missions-Sending Department

What, then, are the characteristics of a mature missions-sending department? A mature missions sending department will have the following ten characteristics:

*1. Long-term missionaries.* A mature missions sending department will have sent long-term missionaries outside of its country who speak the languages of the people they are working with. They will have overcome the barriers of time (short-term only missionaries), distance (just going to near-by nations), language (speaking only the language of the sending country) and religion (reaching people within the same or similar religious context). Each barrier requires a greater effort than the previous.

*2. Income.* Their income is constantly growing, and has possibly even surpassed the income of the general headquarters. You know that you have a mature missions vision when this condition no longer bothers church leaders nor causes jealousy among them. They rather, rejoice that more income is given to missions than to the general administration of the church.

*3. Pastoral care.* The department provides pastoral care to the missionaries in the field. The missionaries are understood and ministered to. This can also be done by local churches. A missions agency should never be seen to take the place of the local church in loving and caring for missionaries on the field.

*4. Executive director.* They have full-time administrative personal with one or more of the executive team dedicated full-time to missions. If the executive director is married to both his church and to the full-time time job of leading the missions department, he will be severely limited in his ability to move the work forward.

*5. Good reputation.* The missions department has a good image and a positive reputation when it comes to the administration of financial resources. Because those administering the finances are transparent in their use of money, there are no legitimate questions about their integrity. There may be some who complain about the amount of money given to missions (which reflects that there is still not a mature missions vision in the church); however, no one complains about the correct administration of those resources.

*6. Savings.* The department is not living day by day but has savings in the bank which will allow it to respond effectively to emergencies.

*7. Decision-making team.* The responsibility of making decisions does not fall on one person only, but there is a team that constantly decides, executes, and evaluates decisions.

*8. English competency.* To ensure that international communication is not limited there is one or more persons in the team who speak English.

*9. Missionary training.* There are training programs to prepare and orient future missionary candidates to the work.

*10. Promotion.* There are programs to motivate and mobilize the churches in all areas, including children, youth, intercessory prayer, promotion, and information sharing to the local churches.

**Steps to Missional Maturity**

Missional maturity is achieved in stages. There are five stages that a missions agency goes through on the pathway to missional maturity:

*1. Pioneer stage.* The beginnings can be slow, but before we are entrusted with much, we must be faithful with little.

*2. Battle stages.* We know of no effective national missions program that did not fight many battles on many fronts with Satan as he tried to stop its advance. Nothing scares the enemy more than the prospect of mobilizing for missions the 95% of our believers who live in the Global South.

*3. Growth stage.* Fruit and permanence are seen as the work progresses.

*4. Consolidation stage.* A solid structure is organized in anticipation of future growth.

*5. Respect stage.* The agency and its leadership has a good testimony in the national church. Though many still do not understand the vision, everyone respects the achievements and testimony of the missions department.

A mature missions department does not necessarily mean that the country has a mature missions vision. It does mean, however, that a mature department will be advancing towards that goal.

Antonio Pedrozo and Brad Walz

# A CASE STUDY: ARGENTINA'S NATIONAL MISSIONS DEPARTMENT

**Historical Review**

The Missions Department of the Argentina Assemblies of God (AAG) officially started in 1983, however, due to frustrating results, it almost closed. In 1989 it was reborn. Then, in 1995, an explosion of new candidates occurred, and in 1997, the *no se puede* (we can't do it), mentality was broken as many missionaries were sent out.

The AAG missions program can be divided into periods. The first period was the time of foundation laying (1989-1995). During that time the foundation was laid for structure and vision. It was a period of missions events, visiting churches, producing materials, preparing and opening a small office, and forming a national missions committee. Soon the first missionaries were sent out. The next period was a time of explosive growth (1995-1998). During these years many who had been previously called came forward, presented themselves to be missionaries, and were deployed to the field.

The third period was a time of consolidation (1998-2004). Following the period of explosive growth, the Missions Department needed to catch up by developing the necessary structures and policies. It was a time of maturing and adjusting to the new challenges. It was during this period that the work faced a great challenge with Argentina's economic collapse and monetary devaluation of 2001. God, however, was faithful and not one missionary was called home. During the fourth period more consolidation occurred with the maturing of the Missions Department (2004-present). The department began to prepare for what we feel is the next wave of missionaries sent out. We have done this by adding more staff and recalling key veteran missionaries to help in the administrative work. This called for more adjustments and changes. New candidates began to go out in 2008-2009. In this missionary group we have more than 180 people called to more than 65 nations.

**Keys to the Foundational Period**

Certain key events and decisions occurred during the Foundational Period of the AAG missions movement. One significant development was that the

Holy Spirit began calling people into missions before a missions department was functioning. This demonstrates the importance of obeying the command of Jesus to "pray to Lord of the harvest to send forth laborers into His harvest" (Luke 10:2). We need to do this for both the present and next generation. Further, the Spirit called a man to lead the movement. The right leader is essential in any successful movement. Sadly, many of the missions departments in the Two Thirds World have failed to develop because they have not yet found the right leader. Some countries have had to change their leaders in order to move forward.

Another key decision of the AAG was to begin emphasizing the "sending call" rather than just the "going call." The major cause for missions failure in many Latin American churches is the failure to develop its sending call. The Holy Spirit has been calling, and continues to call, many young people to the fields of the world. While we rejoice in this, the AAG Missions Department has emphasized a sending rather than a going vision.

A church must also use care in choosing its first missionary candidates. It must send only those who are prepared to go and not try to force the timing by simply trying to send out more missionaries. The right candidates will open the door for others; the wrong ones will slow the program's growth. All along the way, a national missions department must remain flexible in its structure and in how and who it chooses as its missionaries. It must recognize God's call on people's lives and not just their credentials. In the past, a missionary candidate had to be ordained to be a missionary. In Argentina this can take ten years. Opening the structure to those who were not ordained ministers was another key factor in the growth of the Argentina missions movement. Structures need to exist, and they serve a vital purpose in missions; however, structures must serve the purpose of the mission rather than the purpose serving the structure.

The AAG chose a fund-raising system that requires missionaries to visit churches in order to raise their own funds. In Latin America churches want to give to people and not just to offices. They are motivated by knowing who they are supporting. We can call this strategy the "personalization of missions."

**Keys in Developing a Sending Vision**

Keys to developing a healthy sending vision in a national church include the following:

- We must begin by working with the way things are now rather than the way we hope things will be in the future.
- Missionaries and missionary leaders must be willing to go church-by-church to raise funds and instill missions vision in the people. Start with those churches that are open, and then, as others open their doors, move to them.
- Leaders must create flexible sending structures that allow those who are called to not have to look to non-AG structures in order to go to the field.
- Create a network of lay people to spread the vision.
- Require missionaries to itinerate and visit as many churches as possible.
- Take advantage of national, district, and other events.
- Be transparent with finances and produce annual reports for the constituency.
- Take the message to the people by conducting national missions tours.
- Ensure that the Missions Department works closely with other departments to help promote and instill a missions vision.
- Use statistics to challenge the church and make missions a reachable goal for all.
- Involve as many leaders as possible in your national missions structure.
- Create and teach courses on missions, including lessons on the biblical theology of missions and biblical principles of giving.

**Getting Momentum**

If a missions department is to be successful it must generate momentum in the movement. The following strategies can help create the necessary momentum:

- Secure the right leader, and then support him and surround him with the right people.
- Take definite steps to break the poverty mentality in the church. A poverty mentality is an incredible stronghold of the enemy in many of our churches and, therefore, must be challenged and overcome.
- Prepare to face and counter the opposition that will come from pastors who will seek to hinder young people from responding to the call to missions.
- Address the lack of knowledge among pastors and leaders of what is going on in the world. For example, many pastors and leaders sincerely believe that their country is the neediest of all countries. They have no clue of the reality of unreached people.

Other missional challenges that may need to be addressed include the following:

- The challenge of being willing to wait for those who are called to mature to the place where they are ready to go. This can be compared to waiting on the fruit of a tree to mature before picking it.
- The challenge of developing unity among the churches.
- The challenge of overcoming the discomfort that people feel with something new.
- The challenge of discouragement in the beginning.
- The challenge of jealousy after the missions department grows.
- The challenge of bitterness in the hearts of the people who are resisting the missions vision.

We who are promoting missions must learn to maintain a balance in our prophetic voice. We must confront the sin of a lack of mission's vision, but, at the same time, we must do it with a pure heart.

## Organization of the Argentina AG Missions Department

We have sometimes been asked just how the missions department of the AAG is organized. Following is a brief description of the organizational model of the AAG Missions Department:

*President.* The missions department is lead by a President, who is a full-time leader. The President's job description has evolved as the department has grown. For example, in the beginning his job was largely promotional and organizational, centered around forming an effective structure. As the department developed, his work became more focused on the supervision and preparation of missionaries.

*Activities.* The Missions Department has many jobs. Among many other things, it prepares missions materials and promotes the work. It is also involved in communication with the sending base and receipting gifts and offerings.

*Offerings.* Churches and individuals usually designate their offerings for certain individuals. They then give their designated offerings through a centralized national missions account, via their bank or Western Union. All offerings are receipted, and each missionary is notified of all donations to his or her ministry account.

*Missions Committee.* The AAG Missions Department has an Administrative Committee for quick and ongoing decisions, and a larger Supervising Committee that meets every two months and makes the more important decisions.

*Candidates.* The Missions Department processes all candidates who apply to be missionaries. The process takes several months and has evolved over the years as the missions sending structure has changed and matured.

*Categories.* The AAG has a number of missionary categories. This allows for more flexibility in responding to various situations on the field and recognizes unique opportunities (see Appendix 5).

*Promotion.* The AAG promotes missions in many ways. This is done through the production and distribution of missions materials. It is also done through missionaries and missionary leaders visiting churches, teaching in various venues, and presenting at retreats. The missions leaders are also present at every national church event.

*Missionary placement.* Before missionaries are placed in a country with a national AG church, contact is made with that church through the Missions Department. No missionary goes to the field on their own. They are, rather, sent through official channels.

## Four Sending Structure Models

There are many missionary sending structure models. Four currently-used missionary sending models are as follows:

*1. Local church as sender model.* In this model the missionary is sent out by a local church with no involvement from a missions agency. In some countries this may be the only model available. The advantage of this system is that a missionary becomes very accountable to his local church, and does not have the pressure of raising finances. One significant disadvantage to this system is that in developing nations with weaker economies it is very difficult for local churches that are not large to send missionaries alone. As a result, those who are called from smaller- and medium-sized churches in this context may not be able to go. From a receiving church perspective, if several churches have several missionaries in the same country, they become many voices instead of one voice to that country. This can cause confusion and misunderstanding in some national church contexts. The expectation for practitioners of this model is that they deliberately network with the body of Christ in their country of service. Networking in the home country with other senders will also help in the sharing of resources and information that can mutually benefit all.

*2. National department with a pool system.* In this system churches give to a central fund, then the directors of that fund decide it is to be administered. This model is used by the US-based Southern Baptist Convention. There are certain advantages of this system. For example, the missionary has less pressure in raising funds. There are also significant disadvantages. For example, since churches give to a central national office, they do not know their missionaries personally and are potentially less motivated to give. Also, in cultures accustomed to corruption in secular organizations, people are often suspect of central funds and sometimes do not trust one person, or a small group of persons, to administer large amounts of money.

*3. National department with churches giving specifically towards the missionary.* In this system a national structure with a functioning committee or commission makes decisions concerning the approval of missionary candidates and concerning how they are sent and supported. Funds are channeled through the central fund of a missions agency, but, unlike the pool system, offerings are designated to individual missionaries. Normally a small percentage (5 to 10%) of each donation is taken out for the administrative budget of the agency. One advantage of this system is that it allows everyone to participate, and everyone who is called can be considered to go. Churches are more motivated to support the missionary because giving is more personalized, and yet, there is still accountability and structure. A disadvantage of this system is that the responsibility for raising the budget is placed largely on the missionaries themselves. They even have to itinerate to raise funds when they come home on furlough.

*4. National department combines working with a local church.* This is a middle-of-the-road sending structure that may work well in countries with strong local sending churches. The agency approves, coordinates, and serves as a contact to the receiving countries, but the local church has participation and a voice in decisions. Some Latin American and European countries use this model. They have a national missions department yet allow the local church to participate in information gathering and in certain important decisions, if it wants to. The local church, however, does not direct the missionary. In the eyes of the receiving church, the missionary is sent by the department and national church and not just by a local church. This sending structure can be a good middle-of-the-road model for countries with strong local churches or places who doubt the virtue of a missions agency.

This list of models is not exhaustive; nevertheless, it can serve as general guide, since most sending structures will reflect one of these models.

## Advantage of a National Missions Department

We believe that it is advantageous for our emerging AG missions movements to start national missions departments to direct their work. The great advantage of such a structure is that many local churches working together can do much more that a single local church working on its own. There is an additional advantage in the relational structure associated with a denominational network. A denominational structure already has major events, such as the General Council meetings of the AG, that reach and motivate many pastors. A missions department can use such a network to promote missions. An interdenominational structure usually does not have such a ready-made network through which to promote missions.

Another important issue worth noting is the power of positive results. Once a missions movement begins producing positive results, these positive results can be translated into even greater results, which in turn encourages others to get involved. As positive results accumulate, they channel the work of God into what we call "a river of blessings" which in turn avoids "flooding" the work with sincere people who make mistakes while doing it alone.

**The Fruits of a Missions Vision**

There are a number of "fruits" that come through the missionary vision of a national church. These fruits include the following:

- It encourages a generous spirit in place of a poverty spirit.
- People are sent out in fulfillment of God's call on their lives.
- A "we can do this" spirit of confidence is produced in the people.
- A sharing spirit is birthed in the churches, that is, a spirit where people think not only of themselves, but of their church, their country, and the nations.
- The kingdom of God is advanced and God completes His purpose.
- People begin to participate more and more in intercessory prayer. (The only way the "Islamic curtain" will ever fall will be through such concerted intercessory prayer.)
- Economic and spiritual blessings accrue. A church's involvement in missions always results in God's spiritual and financial provision.

## HOW THE LATIN AMERICAN MISSIONS NETWORK HAS HELPED "WEAKER" COUNTRIES.

In the last few years the term *networking* has become popular in US business culture. It is a powerful concept. For example, the World Assemblies of God Fellowship (WAGF) is a huge international network. A few years ago one Latin American missions leader objected to the term. In response, I told him the following story. There is an AG missionary from Bolivia in India. This man's missions department also wanted to send a worker to India. I then put them in contact with the missionary in Bolivia, who, speaking the same language, was able to give them advice based on his own experience, and then put them in touch with the Indian national church leadership. I participated no more in the process. I asked him, "Was that contact positive for you? "Of course," he replied. I responded, "That's networking!" Networking is working together, finding common ground, building bridges, and establishing mutually positive contacts.

**Seven Necessary Missional Networks**

Effective missions work is often carried out through networks, or alliances. Here are seven of those key networks:

*1. God and missionary.* Every missionary career begins with the call of God (Luke 10:2, Acts 13:2).

*2. Church and missionary.* The "going call" of the missionary can only be fulfilled through the "sending call" of the national and local churches (Rom. 10:15).

*3. Church and local missions department.* Every church needs a missions department which is given liberty to function. As well, missions must be more than a department in the church; it must be the vision of the church.

*4. Church and national missions department.* Without an effective national missions department only large churches can participate in foreign missions, and only missionaries from large churches can go. With an effective missions department every church, large or small, can participate, and every missionary, from every place, can go. Therefore, national missions departments and local churches need to network together to see this important alliance work.

*5. Missions departments with other missions departments.* We must learn from each other, especially in the early stages of missions development. For example, all of the twenty Spanish-speaking national churches of Latin American now have missions departments. Thirteen of those efforts are less than three years old.

*6. National missions department with receiving church.* In many cases the AG national church is the strongest work in the country. This happened because of Pentecost and because of strategy, with the North American churches working with, and even submissive to, the national church of a given country. The North American missionaries did not try to raise up a dependent national church. Yet, oftentimes these same national churches fail to respect other national churches when they send out their own missionaries. In 1990 a missions team was sent to Argentina, generously backed by a strong Asian AG church. They refused to work directly with the Argentina Assemblies of God, but said, "We want to work with *the* Church," meaning the church universal. Tragically, in not submitting to and respecting the Argentine national church, they made many unnecessary mistakes, and ended up failing. In wanting to work with everyone, they ended up working with no one. It is important that missions departments understand the importance of these strategic networks, and that they respect the existing national church, submitting themselves to, communicating with, and working alongside of them.

*7. Missionary with missionaries from other Assemblies of God churches.* It is important we do our best to network with each other, and not work independently of each other. Sometimes, Assemblies of God-sent workers, instead of networking with and working with the Pentecostal philosophy and missiology of other Assemblies of God workers, have chosen to network with and submit themselves to non-Pentecostal missions agencies, or agencies which have a very different philosophy of work. Recently an inter-denominational leader from Argentina said to me, "The Assemblies of God is the best network in the world. If I could have access to it, I would not even consider looking to others or thinking the grass is greener on the other side." Sometimes we who have "the best network in the world," envied by many others, fail to take advantage of it.

**Our Latin American Network**

In 1994 the Argentina AG Missions Department began its efforts to establish communications with other Latin American missions departments. In the beginning it was a slow process, since there was a certain fear of each sending agency loosing its autonomy. We were thus very careful to clarify that we did not want to create one big Latin American missions agency. In 1997 we formed the *"Misiones En Conjunto"* ("Missions Together"). There are now two missions bodies in Latin America, the CELAD, with 14 member countries, and the CADSA, with 6-7 member countries. While Brazil is officially part of CADSA, because of the difference in language its participation is minimal. Thus, we united these twenty Spanish-speaking countries into a single missions network. The commission was formally inaugurated in 1998 with Brad Walz of Argentina serving as President.

Our first historical meeting of missions leaders was held in Panama in April of 2000. About 50 missionary leaders from 17 Latin American countries were in attendance. Another historical first conference was held in Guatemala in March, 2001, attended by more than 420 delegates from more than twenty countries. This number included 12 general superintendents and representatives from 15 missions departments from across the region. Since then, the network's annual events gather more leaders from across Latin American than any other AG event. A consultation is held every year and a congress is held every three years.

**Three Pillars of Our Network**

Our Latin America missions network stands on three key pillars, as follows:

*Pillar 1: Communication.* Pillar 1 includes e-mail updates sharing both popular information and leader updates. An electronic journal is planned for the future.

*Pillar 2: Resource Sharing.* Pillar 2 includes informational databases of Latin American missionaries and contacts, missions models and training resources, and unreached people groups.

*Pillar 3: Leadership Consultations.* Consultations are conducted on a yearly basis with a major conference every third year. The consultations and conferences deal with missiological trends and issues. They also encourage natural networking through the relationships built at the conferences. (The Latin American Statement on Cooperation can be found in Appendix 3.)

**The Challenges and Keys to Successful Networking**

One major challenge in networking is multi-national teams. Conflicts between missionaries are inevitable. This is true even among missionaries from the same country and working with the same mission. It is therefore understandable that it will not be easy for missionaries from several countries, cultures, and languages to network together into one unified team. But it can be, and has been done. Three keys to such intercultural networking are communication, respect, and trust.

Missionaries from different countries and cultures come with different philosophies. And yet, though different cultures have different ways of approaching life, there is, most likely, a basic philosophy that all can agree upon. It is essential, therefore, that multi-national missionary teams work out a basic philosophical guideline. In doing this each team member must demonstrate humility and grace. Further, each team member must be ready to learn from the others. Even the most seasoned missionary can learn from the least-experienced one. I often take ideas back to Argentina from countries I have visited. For most of us networking in international teams is uncharted waters. There is thus a certain fear factor involved. We must not, however, fear the unknown, but be being willing to take the risk, realizing that the potential benefits are great.

There is also the challenge of fear of "spiritual imperialism." Many times the dominant missionary force of a country will be western missionaries. In such cases there can be a certain fear of working alongside of them. As well, there can be fear among these same westerners of the unknown challenges of working with missionaries from other countries. Through the years US missionaries have made mistakes, nevertheless, they have ultimately learned to submit themselves to national leadership. As the Two Thirds World missions movements mature, they too will take their place in leadership. We must dare to partner together in international teams. In such teams we must commit ourselves to respect one another and to work together as partners.

## RAISING AND MENTORING MISSIONS LEADERS

Mature, visionary leaders are another key to have functioning, serious, and strong sending structures. But, how can we raise up and mentor such leaders? We can begin by addressing those issues that hinder one's developing into a strong missional leader. Seven of those issues are (1) a misunderstanding of the Great Commission, (2) selfishness, (3) ignorance or lack of knowledge about the world, (4) an independent spirit, (5) a wounded spirit, (6) an inferiority complex, and (7) a poverty mentality. When not addressed and remedied, these issues hinder otherwise potential leaders from hearing the voice of the Holy Spirit. Before a leader can be successfully mentored, he or she must overcome these issues by the help of the Holy Spirit and the missional mentor.

As we seek to raise up new missionary leaders, we must be careful to raise up, not only "goers," but also "senders." Early on in our missions movement in Latin America our problem was that the Holy Spirit inspired a "going vision" through revival, but the church did not respond with a commensurate "sending vision."

In mobilizing the church for missions we must do two equally important things: We must raise up people to go and we must mobilize the church to send. Both are the work of the Holy Spirit. In Argentina we did not call anyone to be a missionary; we left that to the Holy Spirit. We did, however, "pray earnestly to the Lord of the harvest to send out laborers into His harvest." We call this the "Luke 10:2 Prayer." It is true that missions-minded churches will produce people willing to go. A wise church will also proactively raise up people to send. The best way, then, to mobilize a church for going is to instill a vision for sending in the church.

**Raising Up People to Send**

One of the primary tasks of a missions department is to help pastors and churches discover their call to send (cf. Rom. 10:14-15). We must, therefore, seek to raise up missions leaders in every local church. We must raise up pastors with a missions vision, and we must raise up local leaders to help their pastors spread the vision. This task is a process, and will take time.

**Principals of Mentoring and Modeling**

If we are going to effectively produce missional leaders, we must model missional leadership before them. In other words, we must practice what we preach. For example, to produce givers, we must ourselves have passion for giving. Our contagious spirit of giving will then spread to others. It is hard to break the old molds of selfishness that have gripped a people for centuries. We must, therefore, approach the task with a positive attitude. We must focus our attention on those who want change and not be discouraged by those who do not. Further, we must have long term vision and plan. We must run the race with patience.

The Bible teaches the principle of sowing and reaping (Gal. 6:7-8). If future missionaries expect to reap the generosity of others, they themselves need to also learn to sow generously, and they must do that today before they become missionaries. They will thus begin to sow "good seeds" that will someday reap a great harvest. Missionaries should also be taught to have a group vision, that is, they not only work to raise support for themselves but also for the larger group.

**Raising Up Local Missions Leaders**

Not only must the pastor be seen as a missional leader, he must also be equipped to raise up local missions lay leaders. He is the inspirer and must be willing to instill missionary vision into the church. However, while it is essential that the pastor owns the vision, it is not always necessary that he be the chief promoter of the vision. He can allow a local missions committee to perform this function.

In Argentina the national Missions Department has accepted the responsibility of going church by church and helping the leaders to develop a local missions team. Further, we have stayed in touch with these missionary leaders by conducting monthly leadership meetings. It only takes one key person to inspire missionary vision in an entire church.

**Raising Up National Leaders**

Not only will a sending vision require leadership on a local level, including both pastors and lay leaders, it will also require committed leadership on a national level. In building a national missions team, begin looking for individuals who are already effectively doing missions in their local churches, or on a district level. Once you locate such people, recruit them and get them involved in a missions committee or resource group. You can then use them to sow the vision among other pastors.

There are a number of effective ways to sow a missions vision on a national level. For instance, you can begin by casting a large missions vision along with concrete, reachable goals. Show the people that it can be done. Then go from church to church promoting the vision and helping to start local missions departments. Take advantage of national conferences to get the message out. Prepare and widely distribute attractive materials proclaiming the missions vision of the national church and announcing the goals. Personalize the vision by having the missionaries visit churches throughout the country. Conduct a yearly national missions tour in which you take the message to the churches. This can be done through regional missionary events. Finally, if you are going to inspire generous giving from the churches, you must communicate well, report often, and have transparency in all of your dealings.

**A Prophetic Voice and a Pure Heart**

Missional leaders must become a prophetic voice to the church, confronting and challenging it to turn from sin and selfishness to obedience to God. People must understand that their disobedience to Christ's Great Commission is sin. However, as missionaries speak prophetically to the church, they need to maintain pure hearts. They should not allow bitterness or discouragement to fill their hearts. Satan oftentimes takes discouragement and bitterness and uses these vices to thwart our vision and zeal. We must ever be on guard against these vices for they will destroy us and mute our prophetic voice of calling God's people to repentance and obedience.

## HOW STRONGER MISSIONS PROGRAMS CAN MENTOR EMERGING MISSIONS PROGRAMS

In the twenty countries of Latin America, four national Assemblies of God churches have strong programs, six have intermediate ones, nine have weaker or pioneer efforts, and one has no program as of yet. There is no doubt that the four stronger programs have had an effect on the other fifteen. At times this effect is informal, while, at other times it is more intentional.

**Informal Influence**

One way informal influence has occurred is through simple example. As national church leaders observed their sister churches progressing in missions, they were struck by the fact that "it can be done." For example, the AAG's surpassing 100 missionaries in 1997 helped break the "we can't do it" mentality prevalent in many AG national churches. A similar impact occurred in 2009 when the AAG broke the million dollar mark in missions giving. News of those advances impacted all of Latin America. Also, in regional missions conferences those with stronger programs are able to share their successes and failures with those from other national churches. Leaders are able to discuss the keys to the missionary successes—and failures. The annual events, along with the functioning continental network, brings missionary leaders into working contact with one another. This contact often results in informal mentoring. Further, leaders from various countries have developed close friendships which aid in missional mentoring.

**Intentional Influence**

Intentional mentoring occurs among AG missions agencies throughout Latin America in a number of ways. For example, each annual consultation or triennial congress is planned around a carefully-considered theme intended to inspire and influence missionary leaders and their national churches. In some instances newer missions programs have requested a missionary from a mature work to help them get started. In 1998 Argentina sent a missionary to Venezuela. As a result, the Venezuela AG has become one of the four strong programs in the region. They have recently sent one of their own missionaries to Peru to help that national church grow in its missionary potential.

Another example of intentional missional mentoring between national AG churches is the intensive half-day training seminars held in the offices of the AAG Missions Department in 2009 and 2010. Presidents of other national missions departments came to learn from our staff and to see first-hand what we were doing. At the conclusion of one seminar one visiting superintendent remarked, "I have learned things here that I can apply, not just to our missions department, but to our General Council and my leadership within it."

In 2010 our Latin American Missions Network (LAMN) held several two- to three-day intensive leadership training seminars in a number of countries. Now, national churches can request that this program come to their country. The seminar includes teachings on 15 key missional topics. In each seminar a presenter from each of our member national churches shares on two or three topics. Each participant covers his or her own expenses, often being helped by their own country's missions program. It is seen as a way of sowing missionary seed into the missions visions of newer countries.

Yet another way intentional missional mentoring occurs in Latin America is through strategic missions trips. In 2003, for example, 14 Latin American missionary leaders were taken to Turkey and Cyprus. Latinos have also participated in the Islamic Consultations that occurred in 2005 and 2009. These group events have had a significant impact on those who have participated in them.

Every third year the LAMN is required to produce a status report and present it to its constituent members. In 2010 we were able to report that from 2007 to 2010 all 21 of our national churches had been visited by a LAMN committee member. Among the purposes of these visits are ministry and mentoring aimed at enabling national churches to move forward in their missions vision.

A final venue where intentional mentoring takes place is in national church events. Each of the national churches in Latin America have given members of our LAMN committee time to share in national church events such as general councils and special congresses.

**Hindrances of Mentoring**

Before we close our discussion on mentoring, we should list and comment briefly on some of the hindrances that mitigate the effects of missional mentoring among national churches:

- *Pride*. Pride can hinder a national church from being mentored. This includes such attitudes as "what can we learn from them?" Being mentored requires humility and a teachable spirit.
- *Nationalistic spirit*. A strong nationalist spirit can also hinder inter-church mentoring. Such an attitude thinks, "How can someone from that country or region teach me anything?"
- *An unteachable spirit*. We must each be willing to admit that we have something to learn, and that we can learn from one another.

Each of these hindrances must be exposed and dealt with if a church is going to move forward in missions involvement.

## CONCLUSION

A few years ago an African friend said to me, "It is time for Africa to stop talking about missions and start doing it." The truth is, Africa has talked much about missions, and yet, in reality, there are very few functioning programs on the continent. In many cases there seems to be only minimal serious commitment from the people and churches. It could be argued that there is not even one strong foreign missions sending program in the Africa AG. While many countries are doing an effective job of cross-cultural missions within their national borders, the Africa Assemblies of God is not realizing its potential of having a number of strong missionary sending programs, resulting in millions of dollars being given to missions.

I propose that the time has come for Africa to adopt a "Nike Theology" of missions. The famous Nike running shoe brand has become well known for their logo and their motto, "Just do it!" For Africa it is time to just do it. Start with what you have and build from there. Raise up leaders. Raise up missions-minded and visionary churches. Build block by block, little by little, and surely you will see many advances in the coming years. You will see trained missionaries ready to go to the field, missionaries who have been sent to the unreached peoples of the world, countries with strong missionary-sending programs, other countries becoming willing to learn, and generous missions giving by many churches and believers. But you must stop talking and start doing. The world needs Africa. It is time for Africa to *just do it!*

# Missional Mentoring: A Response to Antonio Pedrozo and Brad Walz

ENSON MBILIKILE LWESYA

I admire the openness and condor of Antonio Pedrozo and Brad Walz in their paper, "Missional Mentoring: How National Churches with Strong and Effective Missions Outreaches Mentor Those Without." They have honestly attempted to address the issue of missional mentoring between national missions departments by using models from their own continent, Latin America. Pedrozo and Walz's paper deals with some key missional issues including a theology of mission, essential practices of running missions departments, inter-agency networking, missional leadership, and others. I will not try to respond to all of the issues addressed in their paper, but have taken the liberty, bounded within the nature of the paper and subject matter, to respond in five frames:

1. The Global South church and its cross-boarder missions
2. Leaders and their place in creating vision and maintaining the momentum for missions
3. Identifying the right systems for mission mobilization and sending
4. Networks and global missions
5. Mentoring mission organizations.

**Global South Church**

Over the last twenty years or so the church in the Southern Hemisphere has grown faster and become larger than the church in the North. Indeed, a religious change, pregnant with sociological impact beyond what the world has ever before experienced, is looming on the horizon. Despite the claims of the rapid growth of Islam, statistics reveal that Christianity is growing even faster, and, surprisingly, Christianity is growing faster in the Global South than in the Global North, with Africa at the epicenter of this exponential growth.[1] In a few years time a "typical" Christian will no longer be a Caucasian from the North, but an African or Asian from one of the buzzing megacities of the South.

Scholars and practitioners have coined different terms to describe the rising missionary movement from the nations of the Southern Hemisphere. "Third World Missions" has been a widely accepted term in the past, especially in political and developmental circles. It is historically associated with the economically less developed countries of the world and contrasted with the politically polarized and economically more developed Western Bloc nations (First World) and the Eastern Bloc nations (Second World). This designation, however, is no longer appropriate, since the economic vitality of some countries in the "Third World" surpasses most countries in the "First World."[2] "Emerging missions" is another term being used. However, is it accurate to continue to characterize a movement, which now comprises approximately 30% of the total Protestant missionary force as emerging?[3]

While the designation "Two-Thirds World" is better than either "Third World" or "Developing World," it is not widely familiar, especially outside of evangelical circles.[4] "Majority World" is, in my opinion, a more accommodating term. It refers in very broad terms to Africa, Asia, and Latin America. "Majority World" reflects the essential fact that living in these regions are the majority of the world's population and of the world's Christians.[5] It recognizes the fact that 83% of the world's population lives in developing countries, and that 76% of the world's nations are developing. Alan Anderson cites Barrett and Johnson's statistics, which reveal that there were 1,227 million Christians in Asia, Africa, Latin America, and Oceania in 2004 (62% of the world's Christians), while those living in two northern continents (including Russia) constituted only 38% of the world's Christians. This is dramatic evidence of how rapidly the western share of world Christianity has decreased in the Twentieth Century. Anderson further notes, "If present trends continue, by 2025 69% of the world's Christians will live in the South, with only 31% in the North."[6]

It is not only in terms of numbers that there have been fundamental demographic changes. Christianity's growth is most often found in Pentecostal and Charismatic forms, and much of this growth is among groups independent of western "mainline Protestant" and "classical Pentecostal" denominations and missions.[7] Majority World missions, or the Global South church, represents the newly-formed (and forming) missionary sending organizations among non-Western Christians, located in Africa, Asia, Latin America, and Oceania. The Majority World missions movement has grown at a phenomenal rate. According to some reports, from 1980 to 1988, the movement increased by 22,686 missionaries. This represents an annual growth rate of 13.39% or 248% per decade. This is five times faster than the Western mission movement, which has grown at 48% during the same ten years. This development has great significance for the future of global missions and the global church.[8] The emergence of the Majority World missions bestows on the evangelical missions movement new boundaries of missionary activities and new categories of missionaries.

Pedrozo and Walz do not, however, hide their disappointment that the often laudable, fast-growing Global South church has not produced hard data demonstrating that the South's emerging missionary movement has surpassed the traditional West in number of missionaries sent. This fact is especially evident in Pentecostal movements, including the Assemblies of God. Nevertheless, the question remains, "How will Christianity from the South affect that of the North?" As Christianity is getting stronger in the South, and a great simultaneous people movement is happening from the South to the North, what are the implications for Christian missions?

The paper clearly shows that missiologists from the Global South have had abundant discussions on the reality of the world's unreached and least-reached peoples, and an increased "vision of going" has been created within its constituents. What remains, however, is to have a "sending vision." Such a sending theology is the church's attempt to set up the mechanisms necessary in order to identify, select, train, and deploy missionaries to the field. These mechanisms include a specific organizational philosophy, intrastructure,[9] policies, culture, and other things. Although, Pedrozo and Walz do not address the issue of the philosophical underpinnings of what missions is, it is axiomatic that a sending vision cannot sustain missions activities in the absence of an adequate knowledge of the biblical theology of missions.

## Leaders and the Missions Enterprise

Pedrozo and Walz conclude, and rightly so, that developing a "sending vision" rests on the development of the leadership capacity within a community. They observe that many times a country is ripe for harvest but the right leader has not been formed, or is not willing, or has not been selected to take up the challenge. The formation and operationalization of the missions department is equally a leadership issue. Leaders facilitate the creating, casting, and communication of missions vision.

Leaders not only initiate the process, they maintain the momentum. The inspirational tone of the various Eleventh Hour Institutes conducted across Africa in sensitization and missional awareness[10] has been mitigated by leaders who fail to maintain the process. One aspect of maintaining momentum is efficiency in managing the processes and systems of a "sending vision." This is done by assuring the community of givers of financial accountability and ensuring the sent missionaries of continued support. Leaders of effective missionary sending systems are essential to Africa's move into full participation in the *missio Dei*. Although leaders are different from managers, organizational life reveals that no one is a pure leader and vice versa (Figure 1).

**Figure 1**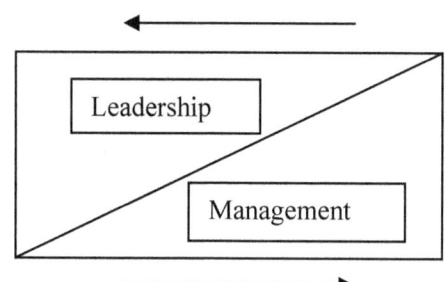

Every leader has a bit of a manager in him, and every manager has a bit of leader in him. In other words, leaders inevitably manifest some form of management skills and managers manifest some level of leadership skills. Thus, in any given leadership team, each member manifests varying levels of each skill. Further, workers in organizations manifest these skills despite their job titles. Effective leadership teams tend to include people with various strengths in relation to leadership and management aptitude. This means the strength of leadership teams depend on a creative inclusion of both leaders and managers as members. Missional enterprise is a taxing and mammoth work demanding creative partnership of various kinds of leaders. Effective leaders, therefore, learn to delegate their weaknesses and maximize their strengths. Africa's leadership would do well to discover their skills, strengths, and abilities. In doing this, they could learn to lead with courage, dignity, and security.

Pedrozo and Walz agree that a huge challenge in developing a missions sending vision and structure is finding the right leadership:

> In country after country, not having the right leader has been an impediment to a structure which many young people and missions-minded pastors yearn for. The great challenge in a church with no missions experience is to have leadership that can guide them towards having their first missions experiences. Across the world, in country after country, the right leadership would speed up the process and growth required for an effective missions sending structure.

Thus, part of the important process in developing missions is identifying and growing leaders with a DNA for missions.

## Structures for Sending Missions

Missions always has a framework through which it is accomplished. By the very nature of its activities, a missionary organization is essential for proper conservation of the fruit of such an enterprise. Pedrozo and Walz recognize four types of sending structures: (1) a local church, (2) a national department with a pool system, (3) a national department with churches giving specifically towards the missionary, and (4) a national department combining work with the local church. The authors identify the fourth model, which they call the "middle of the road," as the preferred structure for denominations with a system of strong local churches like the Assemblies of God.

Pedrozo and Walz state that one success factor to a successful missions enterprise is a strong sending structure. In relation to this they identify three important principles:

1. Everything that is worth something, takes time, thus, attaining maturity in the sending structure takes time.
2. You need the right kind of leaders to champion the establishment of a sending theology and structure.
3. Most of the countries in the sending South are in the pioneer stage and, therefore, a deliberate mindset to mature them is essential.

In Part 4 the authors present the Argentina AG's national Missions Department as one example of a developing sending structure. Their conclusion at the end of Part 3 is very helpful in that it reveals how structures that are well focused and always maturing are most productive in the missionary enterprise. A mature missions department does not always mean that the country has a mature mission's vision. It does mean, however, that the department is advancing towards that goal.

National churches wanting to send missionaries outside their countries must, of necessity, develop clear infrastructural road maps that specify the vision, mission, objectives, goals, and strategies of the enterprise. Further, there must be an organizational infrastructure detailing governance structures, leadership, offices, policies, and procedures. By nature, a sending theology should be flexible, since it must be constantly refined to respond to the ever-changing needs on the field. The trueness of a sending theology shapes the missional practices of the church, such as sensitization, awareness, mobilization, selection, and the training and deployment of missionaries. All of the above must be addressed and defined in developing an adequate sending vision.

Many national churches affiliated with AAGA have missions departments, albeit with differing levels of functionality. The Eleventh Hour Institute and the Acts in Africa Initiative[11] have helped to bring a greater awareness to the church of the necessity of missions done in the power of the Spirit. These two missional organizations have sought to intentionally influence national churches in the development of operational missions departments. Nevertheless, we must admit that most of the missions departments of our national churches in Africa are still in the embryonic stages, and some, unfortunately, are in name only.

## Networks and Global Missions

Pedrozo and Walz recognize the importance of networks in missions, pointing out how they help to "build bridges, work together, find common ground, and work in mutually positive contacts." The fact that no one can survive alone and no one Christian group can win the whole world alone underscores the necessity of missional networks. The authors' discussion on networks includes a description of seven kinds of alliances necessary in missions work: (1) God and missionary, (2) church and missionary, (3) church and local missions department, (4) church and national missions department, (5) missions department and other missions departments, (6) national missions department and receiving church, and (7) missionary and missionaries from other Assemblies of God national churches. Among these alliances, the last three are of great importance and could strengthen collaboratives such as ours who seek to bring together AG missional leaders from across Africa.

After discussing the philosophy and nature of networking, Pedrozo and Walz proceed to discuss the historical development of the Latin America networks. They discuss three essential pillars of their missionary networks: communication, resources sharing, and leadership consultations. The Africa AG has had a similar journey in the development of regional networks created for the purpose of assisting the work of missions. Links between national churches were initially facilitated through the US Assemblies of God World Missions (AGWM), which had a ready-made network of missionaries working throughout Africa. Through deliberate means, using historical events such as the Pan-African Conference on Prayer, the seeds of continent-wide collaboration were sown. A stronger attempt for a whole-African collaborative was birthed with the preparatory meetings for the Decade of Harvest emphasis of the 1990s.[12] In 1989 in Lilongwe, the Malawi Assemblies of God hosted an important continent-wide meeting of national superintendents. This historic meeting set the mood for the now-historic Decade of Harvest. Later, Zimbabwe hosted a larger meeting for ministers from across the continent.

The Decade of Harvest, a world-wide strategy of the Assemblies of God, brought the issues of evangelism and mission to the fore. Arguably, its greatest successes were in the growth of national churches through thousands of new church plants across the continent. During the Decade of Harvest collaborations between AGWM missionaries and individual national churches helped to facilitate the growth of national movements. The Africa Assemblies of God Alliance (AAGA), which was created during the Decade of Harvest, despite its being a loose alliance of national churches and leaders, continues to grow in strength and influence. AAGA's regional networks, that follow AGWM administrative lines, have also grown and matured over the years. Under the visionary leadership of the late John V. York, Africa Theological Training Services (now Africa's Hope), which was formed during the Decade of Harvest as a training agency to work alongside the African church, launched various initiatives that became seedbeds of missional envisioning. ATTS further established guidelines for quality theological education and then provided learning materials for Bible schools across the continent. The Eleventh Hour institute was an initiative of ATTS.

Although I have no historical records of what has happened in the development of networks and missionary work in the various regions of the Africa Assemblies of God during the period, I can vouch for the creative leadership of the Holy Spirit in the development of a missionary vision within the East Africa region. In 1995, a historical meeting of Bible school teachers, administrators, and national leaders from Malawi, Tanzania, and Kenya was held at the Assembly of God Bible College in Dodoma, Tanzania. This was the first of the three powerful missionary meetings of the region. The other two were called Leadership II (Iringa, Tanzania, 1997) and Leadership III (Limuru, Kenya, 2001). Leadership II called for the establishment of the Eleventh Hour Institute and the Regional Missions Board of East Africa (RMB). In 1999 the first ever EHI was held in Lilongwe, Malawi. The EHI was designed to sensitize, mobilize, and deploy missionaries, while the RMB was established to oversee the actual administration of a missionary network within the region and to supervise regional missionaries from participating national churches.

There has never been an independent study on the results of the EHI activities; however, anecdotal evidence reveals some significant positive effects in the areas of missionary awareness, the creation of missions departments in most national churches, and the impact on theological education. Neither have I seen an analytical report on the activities of the RMB, which seemed to have worked well the first three years and later stopped functioning. Its operations epitomize the saying "a public cow dies of starvation." To a certain degree, the RMB did not work out the cultural and national challenges that surface when such networks are created. How does a national church support a missionary who is not their own, and whom they have not seen before? The RMB concept was good, but its leadership needed to do a lot of lobbying and training, especially in relation to leaders of missions departments of national churches in the region. The Latin America network, with only twenty nations and one primary language can potentially grow stronger with less difficulty than Africa, which has fifty nations which are very diverse ethnically, economically, and linguistically. Although AAGA's regional networks are growing stronger every year, reporting, evaluation, and monitoring are not yet embraced as essential for developing an effective culture for missionary implementation. Unfortunately, this is also true for other continent-wide initiatives of both AAGA and AGWM.

**Missional Mentoring**

In the last two parts of their paper Pedrozo and Walz specifically deal with the subject of missional mentoring. They first deal with the need and processes of mentoring missions leaders, stating that they are the "key to have functioning, serious, mature, and strong sending structures." They also deal with mentoring within larger regional networks. The authors recognize that all mentoring is casting influence to others through relationships. Basically, mentoring is a relational experience in which one person empowers another by sharing God-given resources.[13]

One form of mentoring is coaching, and the essence of coaching is listening. Great coaching is artful, compassionate, and incisive. In groups, coaches often act as facilitators helping to create an atmosphere of safety. Indispensable to both mentoring and coaching is the ability to create an example, a model worthy of imitation. These two skills are essential in developing great missional leaders, both in national movements and within regional networks. Pedrozo and Walz present the Argentina AG as a missions model worthy of imitation when they tell of how the Argentine church surpassed 100 missionaries in 1997 and how achieving that milestone helped to break a "we can't do it mentality" in the church. They further testify how "breaking the million dollar mark in offerings in 2009 made another impact within the regional network."

I believe in the efficacy of mentoring and coaching others, including missional leaders. As part of my process of accepting the leadership of the AAGA/WMC, I proposed to the AAGA Executive Committee a stronger level of mentoring and coaching leaders of mission. In that proposal I indicate that we should

> ...adopt that the next level of involvement of AAGA and AGWM in the already established national churches become an intentional process of walking alongside Africa's leaders in establishing stronger missional movements impacting the continent and the rest of the world (missional mentorship). This can be a designed project for a specific time period. Part of the new orientation should be in developing personnel, infrastructure, training, resource mobilization approaches, etc. In this regard, we propose the setting up of a pool of missionary consultants with the capacity for leadership development, administration expertise, and mentoring to give capacity to national leadership structures that so wish. Of course, knowing the sense of sovereignty in the national church structures, the process will work best when national leaders are the ones who ask for such consultants.[14]

Missional mentorship involves mentoring and coaching missional leadership in a specific national church as it implements its missionary vision informed by a thorough understanding of the biblical theology of missions. Although this idea may sound new to many of us, it has already been working in several countries. Argentina, Costa Rica, Tanzania, Kenya, and others have had AGWM leaders help develop the sending structures for their national churches. Thus, the strategy that is being proposed in this paper has already proven itself to be workable and sustainable.

Therefore, one major way to capacitate a national missions department is to allow a leader from another African country, or an AGWM missionary, to act as a mentor to the director, or for that person himself to serve as director for three years or so. This individual should, of course, have the necessary qualifications in terms of vision, passion, and relationships. He should also have a level of competence in the areas of finances, institutional memory, and experience. With proper terms of reference for guidelines, the mentor can help to revamp the infrastructure of the existing missions program and institute a results-oriented culture into the department. Modalities, approaches, and processes for such arrangements could be worked out by ad hoc teams under the supervision of AAGA and AGWM or within their respective regional networks. As I have already noted, Argentina, Costa Rica, Tanzania, Kenya and others over several years have used this form of partnership to a high degree of success.

Creating strong sending structures and proper financial accountability in a national mission department demands time, patience, expertise and humility. The Assemblies of God system of electing missions directors poses one of the biggest threats to such an outcome. This is because an ever-impending election implies the possibility of a change of leadership in the near future. Pedrozo and Walz noted how strong nationalistic pride and lack of a teachable spirit can work against a national church adopting such a strategy. Other hindrances could be lack of a unifying culture, a poverty mentality, and a lack of sense of the lostness of people in the world.

**Conclusions and Recommendations**

The paper of Pedrozo and Walz is to be commended and should be a helpful tool in the development of Africa's Pentecostal mission. I commend it as an orientation tool for national church and missions department leaders. By using Latin America in general, and Argentina in particular, to discuss the various issues regarding the implementation of the *missio Dei,* Pedrozo and Walz are straightforward in admonishing Africa to stop talking missions and start doing missions. They call on Africa to adopt a "Nike Theology" of missions, which demands a "just do it" approach.

Their declaration that the Africa Assemblies of God does not have even one strong foreign missions sending program at first seems a bit over-critical. However, to a great extent, their criticism is correct, even though exceptions may be noted if one takes into account the differing contexts of the Latin American and African churches. Africa is much more diverse in terms of language, culture, and the number of countries, making missional networking between national churches much more complex. There is also the accusation that "nothing" seems to be happening in African missions. However, the truth is that what is happening in Africa often goes unreported, or at best, is inadequately reported to the larger AG communities. This lack of good communications is one significant weakness of Assemblies of God missions networks in Africa. Nevertheless, as one person stated, "You don't destroy a mirror just because your image looks awful." Pedrozo and Walz criticisms, as painful as they may at first feel, should serve to spur the African church to *just do it!*

Based on the explanations, conclusions, and suggestions of Pedrozo and Walz concerning the growth and direction of missions from the Global South church, I make the following recommendations to the WMC:

1. Let the WMC partner with AAGA and AGWM in implementing a contextualized, time-bound missional mentorship program. This is a clear call for select missionaries from AGWM and AAGA-related national churches with strong missions-sending programs to partner with receptive, yet needy, national missions programs as mentors or missions directors.
2. The AAGA/WMC and AGWM should partner together to conduct annual Pentecostal Mission Consultations and triennial Mission Congresses for missions department directors and other key missional leaders.
3. I further call on national AG churches and missions departments across Africa to participate in a continental missions network. In doing this, they should submit annual reports to the WMC regarding their national mission activities. In addition, we should encourage and receive anecdotal reports from across Africa evidencing Pentecostal missions work on the continent. We do this in realization that each missions department has a unique self-identity and understanding, and each one has a unique journey, and therefore, develops differently despite the networks desire for hard data evidencing production and growth.

I once again commend the authors' passion and a clear sense of understanding that the church must have both a vision of going and a vision of sending. Pedrozo and Walz's experience is noticeable throughout their paper, and I pray that those of us who read and reflect on the many issues addressed therein will, with the help of the Holy Spirit, *just do it!* May the Lord of the Harvest grant to the Assemblies of God in Africa the grace—both favor and enablement—to truly participate in sending missionaries to the entire world, even as the Lord matures the work on the continent. In his paper, "Globalizing Pentecost and Missions in Africa," Denzil R. Miller has truly grasped what it will take for the Africa AG to aggressively advance in missions. If leaders at every level and believers in our Assemblies of God churches across the continent will catch the vision of a church empowered by the Spirit and totally sold out to Christ to and His mission, the world could literally be turned upside down.

The emphasis is well placed that "a truly Pentecostal understanding of missions should include, not only a Pentecostal understanding of missions, but a missional understanding of Pentecost." This insight can indeed help to align the movement into one great agenda, the fulfillment of the *missio Dei*. Many times, and in many quarters, the power of Pentecost is sought and valued only for personal gain. The Spirit is sought as a means for personal breakthroughs or as an anointing for the raising of the Christian from a lowly life to a prosperous, healthy, and happy life. The power of the Spirit becomes primarily the answer to the African problems of pain, poverty, misery and disease. Miller is right that a clear emphasis on the missional objective of Pentecost can help in setting our priority.

Miller lays out the challenge, "In true Pentecostal fashion, Africans must be prepared to go, without restriction, wherever the Spirit directs." There is no doubt that the Spirit, as Superintendent of the work of harvest, intends to send Africans to the entire world. The doubt or question arises when one starts thinking about whether the African church is ready to send and be sent, whether the African church is alert enough to prepare itself for such an awesome, unfinished task.

More doubts can arise when we Africans deem ourselves unable to compete with the missions model of Western missionaries. Admittedly, at present our sending base cannot be as structured, or as wealthy, as our friends in the West. And it may take a generation or more to establish a strong sending mentality within our 16 millions constituents meeting in 65,000 local congregations in 50 national churches in the Africa AG. This is where I find Miller's suggestion that we take the missions model of Jesus and the apostles very hopeful. Africa can become a force in the earth, just as did the early church. The social, political, and economic circumstances troubling the early church did not stop that first-century Pentecostal community from carrying out their missionary mandate, and neither should it stop Africa.

ENDNOTES

[1] Philip Jenkins, *The Next Christendom: The Coming of Global Christianity* (NY: Oxford University Press, 2002), 217-220.
[2] Larry Pate, *From Every People: A Handbook of Two-Thirds World Missions with Directory/Histories/Analysis* (Monrovia, CA: MARC, 1989), 12
[3] Ibid., 13.
[4] Chris Wright, *What Do You Mean by the Majority World?* Available on http://www.johnstott.org/CC_Content_Page/0,PTID326046%7CCHID719122,00.html, accessed 28 February 2006.
[5] Ibid.
[6] Alan Anderson, "Towards a Pentecostal Missiology for the Majority World," *Asian Journal of Pentecostal Studies* 8:1 (2005): 29-47.
[7] Ibid.
[8] Pate, 45.
[9] The intrastructure of an organization is the software part of the system. It includes such things as mission, vision, values, and guiding philosophies.
[10] The Eleventh Hour Institute, a mobile mission school started within the East Africa Assemblies of God region, was later adopted by the Africa Assemblies of God Alliance (AAGA) to serve the continent. Although its mandate was to sensitize, mobilize, and train the African missionaries, its greatest strength was in inspiring and raising awareness of Pentecostal missions and Africa's responsibility in that regard. Lazarus Chakwera's doctoral project was, in part, aimed at developing the curriculum for the institute and mapping its initial exploratory session. John V. York, the then Director of Africa Theological Training Services (ATTS) was singularly used of the Lord to help cast and communicate this missionary vision and attempt its implementation under various initiatives under his leadership. The EHI is an initiative under the ATTS Leadership Management.
[11] The Acts in Africa Initiative was mandated by the Africa Assemblies of God Alliance to help inspire the African church to seek God for continent-wide Pentecostal revival in preparation for the greatest evangelistic, church planting, and missionary advance in the movement's history. Denny (Denzil R.) Miller, the organization's pioneer, came to Africa with a conviction that Africa has a place in the missions enterprise of God, and that it can only fulfill its God-given missionary destiny by following the biblical mandate of first being empowered by the Holy Spirit.

[12] A broad-based initiative of church growth, evangelism, and missions operationalized by the Assemblies of God in the last decade of the twentieth century. During that time the African AG grew from about 2 million to 12 million constituents.

[13] Robert J. Clinton and Paul D. Stanley, (1992). *Connecting: The Mentoring Relationship You Need to Succeed in Life*. Colorado Springs, CO: NavPress, 38.

[14] Part of the discussion in the attached proposal.

*Missional Mentoring: a Response*

# Missional Tensions: Theological Training Systems and Compassionate Ministries in African Missions

## WILLIAM KIRSCH

Historically, the church has grappled with balancing compassion and evangelism. In fact, David Bosch, in his highly acclaimed *Transforming Mission,* claims that this issue is "one of the thorniest areas in the theology and practice of mission."[1] The Lausanne Covenant that was adopted by the International Congress on World Evangelization in 1974 included two paragraphs each touching on one of these aspects. Paragraph four, entitled "The Nature of Evangelism," and paragraph five, entitled "Christian Social Responsibility," addressed each of these issues, but they failed to spell out their relationship to each other. Paragraph six does indicate that "in the church's mission of sacrificial service, evangelism is primary."[2] Many evangelical missionaries from a century ago were generally uninterested in anything that was not strictly evangelism, even to the point of classifying training ministries as beyond the scope of the primary task of evangelism. John R. Cheyne quotes Philip Crows at the Islington Conference in 1968 as quoting R. N. Cust "a missionary of the last century, who argued that money for missions was 'collected for the purpose of converting a soul, not sharpening an intellect.'"[3] So, depending on who you are talking to, theological training could fall on either side of the compassion/evangelism debate.

Because of this lack of a definitive statement on the relationship between the roles of evangelism and social responsibility, and a growing divide in the response of various camps on this issue, a Lausanne committee was convened to address specifically the relationship of evangelism and social responsibility.

Out of this committee's work was issued the "Lausanne Occasional Paper 21: Evangelism and Social Responsibility: An Evangelical Commitment."[4] The stated reason for addressing the issue was

> to complete Lausanne's unfinished business and to define more clearly what is included in "social responsibility," whose responsibility it is, and how it relates to evangelism. For many, fear that the more we evangelicals are committed to the one, the less we shall be committed to the other; that if we commit ourselves to both, one is bound to suffer; and in particular that a preoccupation with social responsibility will be sure to blunt our evangelistic zeal.[5]

I was encouraged that the Lausanne Committee for World Evangelization and the World Evangelical Fellowship had, as far back as 1982, taken it upon themselves to address this issue. I was further encouraged to find that "the stated goals of the consultation indicated that we would focus first and foremost on Holy Scripture. We have been determined, therefore, to let our minds be formed not by any human ideology but by the Word of God."[6] However, as I pursued the document for some theological underpinnings on the subject, I found only some steps in the right direction, but not what I would call a "biblical theology of compassion ministry." Although the document fell short of addressing the issues comprehensively, we need to realize that this was likely not their purpose. Nevertheless, the document does contain some help for us. Of particular note is the report's indication of the individual's responsibility in compassionate works based on Matthew 25:

> In this solemn description of the day of judgment, the "sheep" or the "righteous," who are "blessed" and welcomed into the kingdom, are those who have ministered to Christ in the hungry and thirsty, the naked and sick, the strangers and the prisoners. The "goats," on the other hand, who are "cursed" and dismissed to eternal punishment, are those who have failed to minister to Christ in the needy. Whether Christ's "brethren" are his followers in general, as other passages seem to indicate (e.g., Matt. 12:46-50; Heb. 2:10-18), or in particular His messengers, as may be suggested by the "cup of cold water" passage (Matt. 10:9-15, 40-42), or may include the rest of needy humankind with whom Christ humbly identifies Himself, the principal message is the same. As the rest of the New Testament teaches, the dead will be judged "by

what they have done" (e.g. Rev. 20:13), and our deeds will include either the loving service of those in need or a scandalous indifference to their plight. These will be an acid test whether we are true believers, or unbelievers.

Neither of these two passages of Scripture can possibly mean that we can gain entry to heaven by our good works. To interpret them in this way would be to turn the gospel upside down. What they are emphasizing is that, though we are justified by grace alone through faith alone, we shall be judged by those good works of love through which our secret faith is made public.[7]

Although this Lausanne occasional paper gives room for a broad definition of who constitutes a "brothers of mine" in Matthew 25, this is a matter of debate even among conservative Christians. A "Compassion Statement" issued by the Assemblies of God World Missions Executive Committee in 2003, gives what I believe to be, a very helpful explanation:

> In the light of surrounding Scripture, "the least of these brothers of mine" (v. 40) is best taken to mean the disciples or other believers, especially those who are impoverished as a result of their sharing in Christ's mission of preaching the Gospel. Matthew 5:19 issues the same word (Greek, *elachiston*) of the "least in the kingdom of heaven." Paul uses the same word in first Corinthians 15:9, "I'm the least of the apostles." Matthew 11:11 uses a synonym (Greek, *micron*) of the "least in the kingdom of God." Luke 12:32 says, "do not be afraid, little *(micron)* flock, for your father has been pleased to give you the kingdom." These passages point to the least ones of Matthew 25:40, 45 as being believers. Further, the fact that all three synoptic gospels, Matthew 12:48-50, Mark 3:35, and Luke 8:19-21, show that Jesus identified His followers as His brothers means that this truth is important. In addition, Matthew 10:37-42 uses similar vocabulary within the context of feeding those who are in need because they preach the gospel. "He who receives you receives me.... And if anyone gives even a cup of cold water to one of these little ones because he is my disciple, I tell you the truth, he will certainly not lose his reward" (vv. 40, 42).[8]

Although this document does not rule out compassionate acts to unbelievers, it does indicate that our primary responsibility is to the household of faith. This same document also correctly points out the individual responsibility of each believer in works of compassion:

Compassionate ministries should encourage local believers throughout the world to take care of the physical needs of believers on a local level, especially those who may be impoverished as a result of the testimony they have borne for Christ.[9]

This statement is in keeping with the Assemblies of God World Missions decentralized approach to compassionate ministry. They have no single agency through which compassionate works are channeled but rather indicate that their network of over 200,000 local churches is the means by which the compassionate touch is delivered to our needy world.[10]

Having given a bit of background on the tension between evangelism and social responsibility in the church, it seems to me the "tension" in my given topic is a good place to begin. Is there a tension between theological training systems and compassionate ministries? If so, what is the nature of the tension? I would first like to establish that tension is not necessarily a negative term. My brother, a civil engineer, tells me that in construction, whether it be a building or a bridge, a good amount of structural tension is engineered into the structure so that the integrity of whatever is being built will be maintained. Tension holds two opposing forces in balance. These two opposing forces can be, and often are, complementary, such as the guy wires and the deck of a suspension bridge. One would be rather pointless without the other. Tension can bring balance.

How does this apply to theological education and compassion ministries? Historically the Assemblies of God has been big on training. Africa Regional Director Mike McClaflin has stated on more than one occasion, "If all our missionaries were forced to leave Africa the last one out would be a Bible school trainer." However, the reality is that the number of new missionaries who become involved in Bible school training is declining. In 1900 when only 5% of Christians were non-Western, this was not a critical issue. Today, with over two-thirds of Christians living outside the West, it has created a huge demand for training in the Majority World.[11] These numbers alone speak to the magnitude of the training need on the continent of Africa. Dr. Tokunboh Adeyemo, for many years the leader of the Evangelicals in Africa, has often been quoted as saying, "The Church in Africa is miles wide and inches deep." Lesser known is his statement, "Africa has been evangelized, but the African mind has not been captured for Christ."[12]

The tension arises when one juxtaposes a huge training need with the massive humanitarian need on the continent. One only needs a nascent understanding of the Gospels to realize that the ministry of Christ exemplified a strong compassionate touch. As the Lausanne documents point out, Matthew 25 speaks to the fact that we will be judged according to the depth of our compassion for human need. I have preached from this passage—often. The focus of my preaching is both on the need for personal involvement in compassionate acts and the ubiquitous "elephant in the room," that is, the realization that the immense human needs of Africa can only be given a scratch on the surface with our current efforts. My measured response is to focus on creating more capacity through Bible school training. Building capacity through training more workers, who will be able to teach others, as 2 Timothy 2:2 instructs us, seems to me to be a logical solution to a great variety of humanitarian and ecclesiastical needs. If we only look at the immense human need, and not at building capacity to respond to this need, we will be in a dangerous position.

There is a general human tendency to attempt to compartmentalize life. I was exposed to this in a magnified way living in South Africa under apartheid. It was a system under which injustice was rationalized largely by the Dutch Reformed Church.

> Some of the most brutal racists who worked for the government were some of the most loyal members of the Dutch Reformed Church, deeply committed to their local communities and profoundly loving toward their families and fellow church members. For example, men were able to justify being loving, faithful husbands and fathers at home (and in their churches) while on the job as national security police they threatened their black neighbors in savage ways. They lived this way by compartmentalizing their lives into a private sphere where their Christian commitments could rule and a public sphere where the demands of their faith took second place to the demands of their own racial/ethnic community and homeland. This compartmentalization justified violent, profoundly unchristian acts against fellow creations of God, even fellow members of the body of Christ.[13]

As we look at issues of compassion and justice I want to avoid what may be a tendency to compartmentalize compassion ministry. Cheyne has aptly pointed out that "if the incarnational agent is to be true to the spirit of our

Lord, the gospel must first of all become incarnate in the life of the proclaimer."[14] As I will show later, this removal of compassionate acts from our everyday life has left the church with an inadequate expression of Christ's heart. I believe we should look at compassionate ministries and theological training as a unified whole, complementing and assisting one another, the result of which will be greater ministry effectiveness.

While Assemblies of God missions has been involved in training from some of its earliest days on the continent of Africa, by contrast, it has been more recently that the Assemblies of God has placed a greater focus on compassionate ministries. While it has always been a part of our makeup, in the past it was often suspect, for fear of drifting into a "social gospel." However, in recent years it seems not only to have lost its stigma, but has taken the forefront in a good number of local church missions initiatives.[15] This relatively recent move has not been without a certain amount of trepidation from a number of those in the ranks. In fact, according to JoAnn Butrin, as recent as the late 1990's, the use of terms like "holistic" and "humanitarian" were deemed as inappropriate for use within US (AGWM) missions:

> When our mission finally did become intentional about sending missionaries to do compassion ministry assignments, there was still much disagreement about what priority that [sic] should receive. There was also uncertainty as to how it should be documented and recorded as part of her missiology. And we were divided in our views of what constituted holistic ministry. I recalled a meeting where almost an entire day was spent by some fifty people debating whether the word *holistic* could even be used in our context. Ultimately, it was decided that it had too much baggage and should not be used, and they chose the phrase "ministry to the whole person." The same discussion occurred regarding the term *humanitarian*, and it was also not chosen as a term to be used in our documentation. These discussions were being held in the late 1990's, not that long ago.[16]

It seems to me that the US Assemblies of God has more recently come to a point of understanding that both are equally necessary components of a balanced biblical world view and both are in keeping with Jesus' desires expressed in His prayer in John 17. He prays that we remain in this world (v. 15). As we remain in this world, we inevitably come into contact with people who need His compassionate touch. However, He also prays that His followers be sanctified by the truth, which He points out in His words (v. 17). This would imply knowing His word and applying its truths, which seems to me to indicate that knowledge or study of His word is necessary.

So, what are the touch points between the perceived tension between theological education and compassion ministries? After asking several if they felt there was a tension between theological education and compassion ministries, I narrowed the focus to four areas that were variously suggested as touch points of tension. I will state these four here and then deal with each in succession:

1. *Theologically:* With the importance of theological training in Africa today, should we emphasize compassion ministry at all?
2. *Missionary Presence:* With the present difficulty many missionaries are having raising their budgets, should funding compassion ministry take a back burner to a perceived greater priority of placing more missionaries on the field? Secondly, many new missionaries are going to do compassionate work, rather than being involved in training ministries. Will this emphasis lead to deficiencies in our foundational work of training?
3. *Funding Priority:* With the current appeal of compassion ministries to the US donor base and the huge training need on the continent of Africa, how can we balance the need for financing theological training with the overwhelming appeal of compassionate work?
4. *Delivery Systems:* How do we package compassion ministry on the continent? Should compassion ministry funding be coupled with theological training and/or evangelism efforts?

**Theologically: Should compassion ministry be left aside to focus more on theological training?**

My first reaction to this question was surprise that it would be voiced. However, as I began to look more closely at the intent behind the question, I determined that it was a question that needed to be voiced because it is the starting place for determining our responsibility. The question caused me to look more deeply at the biblical narrative to determine what, in management terms, is "standard biblical policy" when it comes to compassion ministry. What does the Bible teach us about when, where, how, and to whom compassion should be expressed? This will be the main focus of this paper. Once a theological base is established, the following three questions are more easily addressed.

Byron Klaus has said, "Evangelicals (including Pentecostals) have an inherent tendency to over simplify complex issues, including teachings of Jesus on the kingdom of God."[17] This tends to be true with regard to our subject—it is a thorny issue. My first exposure to the tension our subject addressed was as a missionary in Botswana in 1984 where I went as a young man to teach in the Assembly Bible School. I spent much of my time in the classroom with twelve eager ministerial students who wanted to do their best to "present themselves to God as approved workers who did not need to be ashamed and could correctly handle the word of truth" (2 Tim. 2:15 paraphrased). However, after leaving the cloistered campus, I came face to face with what all of us who live in Africa face, the overwhelming human need. One of the first Tswana phrases I learned was, *Go maswe go kopa madi,* translated, "It's not nice to beg for money." It was a tension between my primary reason for being in Botswana and the pressing human need.

This juxtaposition is not new to the church. Jesus' own life and ministry often had touch points with this tension. In fact, the world Jesus lived in is not that different from that in Africa today:

- Ubiquitous human need
- Uneducated poor
- Political and religious elite.

An additional insight from my time in Botswana lends light on what I will later highlight as a biblical pattern. As part of the program at the Bible school, we would take students out on weekend ministry for practical application of what they were learning in the classroom. I remember one weekend in particular in the village of Molepolole. It was a typical weekend of evangelism in the village: preaching, praying for the sick and inviting the lost to receive Jesus, or at least attend church on Sunday to investigate Christ's claims. This particular weekend as the students were moving about the village, challenging people to follow Christ, they prayed for an old man who had been crippled for many years. The man was instantly healed. As I preached on Sunday morning, there was standing room only with many looking in through the windows.

Word had made it around the village that the old man had been healed. Many were there to see for themselves. Indeed the old man was there running up and down the aisle and many responded to the call to salvation that morning. This is an example of what I call "compassion on the way." As the students were going about the activity of reaching the lost, they prayed for a crippled old man, and the compassionate touch of Jesus healed him.

What is the biblical model? How do we recognize our Savior as our model relates to compassionate ministry? What pictures do the gospels portray? Jesus taught His disciples how to minister through walking with them and teaching them power ministry through His example of touching and healing those in need. I often teach my students that any evangelistic effort should be accompanied by praying for the sick. Signs and wonders in the book of Acts were twice as often done before unbelievers.[18] Its benefits are twofold as the healing is both an expression of Christ's compassion and a sign to the unbeliever of His power. It must be noted that the kind of compassion Jesus expressed in His ministry was mainly through powerful works of healing.

> While it is not wrong to note that Jesus had compassion to touch the untouchable of society, the point often missed by those advocating compassion ministries, is the miraculous. To replace the significance of the miracles of the New Testament with simple compassion, touch, or medical assistance is to misinterpret the miracles. Rather, integral mission should include the miraculous.[19] "Surely, Christian transformation should aspire to the same—word, deed, and sign."[20]

It seems to me that the academic community should, rather than see compassionate ministry as something that removes potential finance from their coffers, embrace compassionate ministry as an opportunity to mentor students in effective ministry. Not only should academics lead their students more in the area of compassion ministries through practical training, but those involved in compassion ministries should become more involved in the academy by using their gifts to train present and future ministers in the intricacies of how their church can be an effective light in their community by embracing the needs of the people who live within the reach of their church.

In Matthew 22:37-40 Jesus responded to a question from one of the theologians of His day who asked Him what is the greatest commandment? He answered: "Love the Lord your God with all your heart and with all your soul and with all your mind…and secondly, Love your neighbor as yourself." Allow me to use this as my starting point. It seems to me that we run into difficulty when we follow one of two extremes:

1. Addressing mainly the first commandment by simply theologically defining it very well, and in doing so, feel we have finished the job.
2. Focusing wholly on the second as a substitute for doing the first, a kind of "works righteousness" whereby, through serving those in need, we feel we have sufficiently shown our love for God.

In the above text, this theologian, who also happened to be a lawyer, in form true to his profession, asked Jesus to clarify by identifying who his neighbor was. Jesus' response was to give us the Parable of the Good Samaritan. In its simplest form this parable tells us that we cannot meet everyone's needs, but we can and should meet the need of the one in front of us. The lawyer's question to Jesus was based on holding tightly to what this world has. Jesus' response tells us that love responds to human need to the best of our ability wherever we find it, what I am calling "compassion on the way."

The problem with "compassion on the way" is that one must have a heart of compassion and be willing to take side trips. In a well-known study conducted at Princeton Theological Seminary in 1970, seminary students were given the task of delivering a speech in another building across campus. Some of the students were told their speech was an orientation speech for new students. Others were told they were to lecture on the story of the Good Samaritan. Another variable was the urgency of the speech; some were told that they were to give the speech in just a few minutes. Along the way an actor played the part of a "victim" slumped in an alleyway. The study showed that the content of the speech had no effect on whether the subject stopped to help the victim.

However, the amount of perceived time had a greater effect as to whether the seminarian would stop and help. Beyond the obvious concern that a seminary student would not stop to help a victim on their way to give a speech about the Good Samaritan, this study tells us that, if we are going to help people as Jesus instructed us to, we must be willing to slow down to take the necessary time to do so.

It is noteworthy that Jesus did not open a school to train leaders for the church He was about to establish. Rather, He called the Twelve, and the Seventy, to follow Him and went about touching people's needs, all the while training His followers in His mobile "school of ministry" (Mark 1:17). Jesus' ministry was an itinerant ministry, never staying long in one place but moving around preaching and healing (Mark 1:38). Jesus' methods and ministry were not embraced by the theologians of His day. The tension can be seen as early as Mark 2 where the theologians questioned the legitimacy of Jesus forgiving the paralytic's sins (v. 6). They were correctly judging the theological validity of a man's ability to forgive someone's sins, but overlooking the fact that Jesus was no ordinary man.

A second early encounter between Jesus and the theologians is found just after He called a tax collector to be His disciple (Mark 2:14). One can visualize the tension swelling as a result of this choice on Jesus' part. Again, the theologians, in a self imposed paroxysm of theological correctness, question His choice of company. Somehow, Jesus wanted to be with the sick and the sinners. It is notable that the only people Jesus condemned were the Pharisees and Sadducees. This condemnation was mainly for their hypocrisy. They were self-righteous and gave alms to the poor only for "show." Holiness and hypocrisy are not difficult to distinguish.

A few verses later there seems to be a groundswell of popular opinion that sides with the theologians, as now "the people" call to question Jesus' spirituality in that John's disciples and the theologians' disciples were fasting while Jesus' were not (Mark 2:18). Then the theologians themselves challenge the spirituality of Jesus' disciples: "Look, why are they doing what is unlawful on the Sabbath?" (2:24). It seems to me that we can quickly go wrong in our theological training if we are overly concerned with the letter but not with the spirit of the law.

Beginning in Mark 3, Jesus begins to take an offensive posture with the theologians. Here He makes a very public statement that human need is more important than the letter of the law. He pointedly confronts the theologians with a decision: were they going to hold to the letter of the law over having compassion on a person in need? In one of the few times recorded that our Savior became angry, Jesus was "deeply distressed" at their stubbornness. It was at this point that the plot was cast for Jesus' betrayal and death, because the theologians of Jesus' day could not recognize their compassionate Savior (Messiah) when He was standing in front of them.

In answer to the concern on the first level of whether the church should be involved at all in compassion ministry when there is such a pressing need for theological training, I think we would be hard-pressed to justify a response that would disqualify compassionate ministry as a vital and necessary part of the ministry of the church. However, this responsibility should first and foremost be an individual rather than a corporate one. It is clear from God's word that believers will be judged, at least in part, on how they respond to the needs of others (Matthew 25:31-46). How then does individual responsibility translate into the corporate responsibility of the church? From a theological perspective the starting point must be to ask, "What is the biblical model?"

Because I have spent most of my adult life in theological education, and have only a basic understanding of compassion ministry, I am not in a position to speak authoritatively on the many nuances of compassionate work. Because of this lack, I did pursue a basic understanding of the theology of compassion ministry. After scanning several books on the subject, I found that most of these books address the practicalities rather than the theology of compassion ministry. Most of these books give some foundational Scriptures that reference biblical passages that address justice, the poor, and the needy; however, they do not attempt a thorough theology of compassionate work. The typical practitioners of compassionate ministries tend not to be biblical scholars, nor do we expect them to be. This is not a problem; however, those who are capable of offering a biblical theology of compassionate ministry need to come alongside the practitioners to give a theological foundation upon which compassionate work can stand.

I was initially encouraged when I found a book entitled *Compassionate Ministry: Theological Foundations* authored by a professor at a well-known evangelical school. After reading the book I was disappointed to find a blatant disregard for standard hermeneutical principles in favor of a clearly biased liberation theological approach. The author asks the reader to jump in "feet first" rather than "head first" by a commitment to using one's imagination when developing theology for ministry, and then allowing our spirituality, derived from ministry, to drive our theology:

> What this book asks the reader to do is to consider jumping into that circle with a specific kind of commitment; a commitment to those who suffer, a commitment to those who lacked dignity and are treated inhumanely, a com-

mitment to those who are locked out of our society, a commitment to the victimized.

This request is not the typical one made by theologians to their audiences in the tradition of academic theology over the past 200 years. Modern theology has, both for good and for ill, been a product of the Enlightenment, the heir of the scientific method, the glory of impartial reason and unbiased investigation. "Just the facts, please!" To ask people to deliberately be biased upfront runs against the grain.[21]

My disappointment was immense. I wanted, yea verily, needed someone who could offer me a clear and concise theology of compassion ministry. Instead, I got a "view from below":

... theological claims have a way of being bound up with and lending support to oppressive structures in society. Viewing our beliefs from below can help us cut through this ideological use of the Christian faith to support and rationalize the interests of the powerful and wealthy and show how practically incredible such claims are. The view from below can accomplish this (1) by providing an alternate interpretation of the Christian witness in Scripture that, in many ways, is closer to the meaning expressed by the original witnesses; and (2) by providing an alternate interpretation of human existence that, in many ways, it is closer to the way things really are.[22]

Thus the author asks the reader to allow him to build a theology of compassionate ministry, not on Scripture and sound hermeneutical principles, but rather on "a prior commitment to those who suffer deeply in our world, then, yield[ing] both theoretical and practical consequences for the development of a theology of ministry."[23] He then takes a standard neo-orthodoxy approach by deriving a theology of ministry based on the existential meaning of who God is or "who is God for us?"[24]

While I applaud this author's desire to address a theology of ministry that adequately addresses the compassionate needs in our world, I believe this can be done without damage to sound hermeneutical principles and a loyalty to God's inerrant word. If our theological education is about training for ministry, what should ministry look like? Our theology should inform, even mold, our ministry practice. However, this is not always the case. Theology has a penchant to get stuck in theory and not move into practical action, for which the theological education is proposed. If our theological education in Africa is to be of value, it must remain a theology that "goes somewhere." For those of us who work with theological education in Africa, we generally agree that our theology—a theology that "goes somewhere" —is inextricably tied to the mission of God or the *missio Dei*. If the *missio Dei* is our aim, it would be prudent to define what the mission of God includes.

The question must be asked, "Is our practice of compassion ministry an outgrowth of a well-informed theology, or is it a practice looking for theological backing?" It is my opinion that the latter will naturally happen if the former is not practiced with intentionality. I would add that this must not be a static model, for once our theology has informed our practice, our practice must be the laboratory that causes us to reflect back on a theology. This is how I intend to approach this "tension" of the subject at hand. My purpose is, not only to forward some theological principles that I feel relate to compassionate ministry, but to allow the models in use to reflect back on our theology.

In all of this, I do not want to lose sight of the creative process, for our creative God can take our theology and practice and shape it into something new that increases our ministry effectiveness in magnificent new ways. Theory informs practice, as it should, and practice can also inform theory in the sense that it forms the context in which we think and believe. Everyone believes something and those beliefs are formulated out of experience. No one can claim their beliefs were formed in a vacuum. Our beliefs drive our actions.

## Compassionate Ministry "On the Way"

When one looks for biblical examples of compassionate acts, it quickly becomes apparent that caring for human need was typically done "on the way." Jesus ministered help and healing to people in need as He was moving about the activities of His ministry. The example Jesus gave of the Good Samaritan was compassion expressed by one who was going somewhere else (Luke 10:25-37). He did not set out with the intent of being involved in an act of compassion, but as he encountered the need, it became a part of His activities for that day.

Further, it can be established that Jesus did not meet every need He encountered. Peter and John were going about their daily activities as they entered the temple (Acts 3). They passed by a crippled man Jesus had likely walked past many times. They offered healing to the man in Jesus' name, not as a preplanned event, but in the midst of their daily routine. I like to think of this as the mission of God within the mission of God. As we go about the work He has called us to do, which is captured in the Great Commission, we do it in a manner that is marked by what we are, which is encapsulated in the Great Commandment. It might be stated,

> *Because of your love for Me,*
> *go to the nations and make disciples by baptizing them,*
> *and teaching them to obey my commands,*
> *and, as you go, love them as you do yourself.*

As I formulated these thoughts, I found myself going back and forth as to which of these two directives is primary. In fact, I rewrote this section several times, emphasizing one then the other. I believe God helped me to come to understand that both are primary and they are to be held in balance:

- **Our Mission:** *Reach the lost ... mature them ... teach them to obey*

- **Our Manner:** *Show the love of Christ ... in Christ's compassion*

**Commandment:** *Manner: What we are, our DNA, identifies us.*
- *Love the Lord completely*
- *Love others unconditionally (as we love ourselves)*

**Commission:** *Method: What we do, our RNA, transmits.*
- *Make Disciples (training them for ministry) Through ...*
- *Baptizing them (bringing them into the church)*
- *Teaching them to obey (maturing them)*[25]

This teaching can be charted as follows:

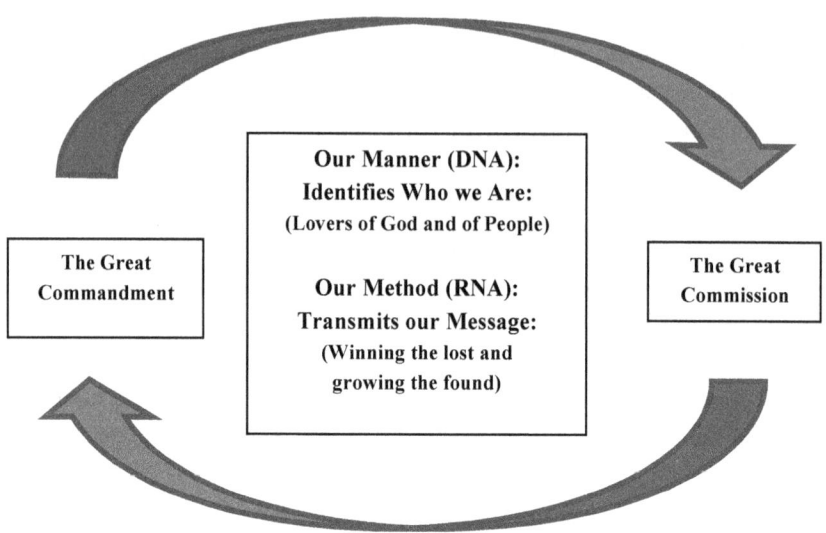

It seems to me that we get it wrong if we reverse this. The Great Commission does not say, "Go into all the world and feed them." If we make compassion what we *do* and make our mission what we *are*, it causes our priorities to become reversed. We reduce the commission of God to a commandment (making it law) and replace the commandment as His commission (making love primary).[26] The end result of this can be the smug feeling that as long as one keeps the commandment, the commission has been fulfilled; or conversely, if you have fulfilled the commission it automatically identifies you as a keeper of the commandment. (I believe we can all identify those who have gone about baptizing and teaching but did not demonstrate the love of Christ as they were "on the way.")

This is an area of great concern and seems to be a growing practice in the church. The manner in which compassion is expressed by some in the church can be a substitute for obedience to the Great Commission *and* the Great Commandment. The church must teach the difference between having compassion and giving funds for the poor. Giving funds for the poor, in the minds of those giving, can replace or become a substitute for having compassion. A believer hears about a humanitarian need somewhere in the world, and expresses their action by placing a gift in the collection to "help those poor people," while at the same time walking past genuine need in their own community. This is not the biblical model.

In Scripture, compassion is expressed directly, from the compassionate person to the one in need. This gives that personal touch that becomes Jesus' hands extended. It is the natural tendency for churches to become inwardly focused. Howard Snyder has well stated, "Church people think about how to get people into the church; kingdom people think about how to get the church into the world. Church people worry that the world might change the church; kingdom people work to see the church change the world."[27]

When it comes to compassion ministries, this means its first place is individual acts that have true meaning in relationship. This is not to say there is no place for compassionate outreach ministries; however, when this becomes a substitute for the believer "expressing compassion in relationship" it leaves the believer feeling as though he or she has done their part by a community compassion event or by putting their financial gift in the offering plate, absolving them from any need of being in relationship with a needy person or in direct compassionate touch. It seems to me that a good theology of compassion will address the individual believer's direct involvement in acts of compassion that become Jesus' hands extended, and places the individual in relationship, which becomes a more meaningful act.

How does this balance of commission and commandment line up with the practice of the New Testament church?[28] Is the New Testament practice more typically one of corporately collecting offerings to send for humanitarian need, or is the pattern conversely that of sharing the gospel while intermittently assisting with human need as it is encountered?

There are three examples in Acts of the church corporately responding to a physical need. All three were in response to a need represented in another part of the body of Christ (Acts 2:44-45; 4:32-35; 11:27-30). The first two provide examples of believers sharing their possessions among other believers who were in need so no one would be in want. In the third Agabus prophesied a famine over the entire Roman world. In response, the disciples in Antioch collected an offering for the believers in Judea. This is the first recorded act of the church after they were "first called Christians." The unique thing about this relief effort was that it was collected in advance of the prophesied need. It is noteworthy that all three recorded cases of the early church responding to compassionate/humanitarian need in the form of a relief effort were believers responding to the needs of other believers.

What then was the norm in the gospels and in the New Testament letters? As has been previously stated, Jesus' model was to assist with needs as He encountered them in His daily activities. Likewise, in the epistles we do not see compassion ministry in the form of relief and development. However, we do see a pattern of meeting needs as they were encountered "on the way." It is this immediate response to human need, as directed by the Spirit, that seems to be the New Testament pattern for compassionate ministry. Although space does not permit an exhaustive exposition, let me point out a few salient examples:

- Matthew 9:35-38: Jesus had an itinerant ministry. As He went, He had compassion on the crowds. His compassion was mainly focused on their spiritually lost condition, and his response was a call for more workers.
- Matthew 10:42: Jesus statement, "If anyone gives even a cup of cold water to one of these little ones because he is my disciple, I tell you the truth, he will certainly not lose his reward," can signify that even a small gift, if it is all one has to offer, will be rewarded.
- Matthew 14:13-21: Jesus, while on the move, expressed His compassion for the crowd through healing the sick and miraculously feeding them.
- Matthew 15:29: Jesus, again in itinerant ministry, expressed compassion by healing the sick. Of interest, is the fact that the people had been without food for three days before He miraculously fed them.
- Matthew 20:29-34: Jesus, on His way from Jericho, healed two blind men. Of note in this instance is the fact that it was the men's persistent cry for help that prompted Jesus to respond with compassion and healing.
- Mark 1:40-42: Jesus responded with the compassionate healing of a man with leprosy only after the man, on his knees, begged for help.
- Mark 6:30-44: After Jesus and the disciples attempted to escape the press of the crowds, the crowds followed them around the lake. Jesus' compassion was at first directed at their spiritual condition and took the form of teaching them. Only later was His compassion expressed

in miraculously feeding them. And, when He did feed them, the bread did not multiply until they began to hand it out.
- Mark 11:12-18: Jesus cleared the temple. I include this incident to point out that Jesus did not always show "compassion." It is thus important to note to whom He did, and did NOT, show compassion, and why.
- Mark 12:41-44: The widows offering begs the question, "Does Africa actually give more than the West?"
- Acts 10:4: Cornelius is commended for his gifts to the poor, and they are considered an "offering before God." Of note here is the fact that these gifts were not necessarily given to believers, since Cornelius was not himself yet considered a believer, but a follower of Judaism.
- 2 Corinthians 1:3-4: God comforts us *in* our troubles, rather than *removing* them.
- Philippians 2:1-4: Our compassion should be modeled after Christ's, which was expressed through humility.
- Colossians 3:12: God's people clothe themselves with compassion, along with kindness, humility, gentleness, and patience.

God's compassion is often linked with His mercy and justice. Mercy is more often related to the forgiveness of trespasses, as it is physical relief. It is notable that often Jesus did not act until a request came to Him for mercy; often in the form of a passionate plea (Matt. 9:27; 15:22; 17:15; 20:30–31, Mark 10:47–48; Luke 18:38-39). Luke 1:50 indicates that His mercy is extended to those who fear Him. The story of the Good Samaritan gives us an example of how mercy should be expressed (Luke 10:25-37). After offering this poignant example, Jesus tells his followers to "go and do likewise." Later Jesus gives another example of how mercy is experienced in the kingdom of God (Luke 18:13-14). It was not given to the theologian who felt smug in his own righteousness, but rather to the tax collector who, out of his spiritual need, begged for mercy. It is not clear in these two examples, but they were likely not what would have been considered spiritual "brothers," so we cannot say that compassionate acts must always be to the "household of faith."

In reviewing the biblical record, it is remarkable how often compassion and mercy are offered only after a passionate plea by the person in need. It is out of recognition of their own need that a compassionate touch is given. Those who work with alcoholics and drug addicts often speak of the need to "raise the floor" on their need. By this they mean bringing the person to the point of their own recognition of their need to change. Raising the floor is arranging circumstances to bring them to their end more quickly, before they severely damage themselves. It has been documented in countries like El Salvador and elsewhere that the message of salvation has created a "gospel lift." Following a Christian lifestyle has removed sinful practices that create continual cycle of defeat and despair. Although, in many cases, the victims—especially as it pertains to children—are not the cause of their own need, the sinful ills of the society in which they live has created the unjust situation in which they find themselves. With this in mind, we must take care in our compassionate acts not to "lower the floor" and thus allow individuals to continue in a lifestyle that continues to devastate their life and keep them in need.[29]

Today the issue the church is facing with compassionate ministry "on the way" is that we are much more "on the way" than ever before. The global village continues to shrink, with a disastrous event anywhere in the world immediately gaining international attention through the media. On our way from the kitchen to the bedroom, the world's compassionate needs meet us on the television newscast. This creates a unique set of circumstances that we face today, one that has never been a part of the picture prior to the twentieth century. On the one hand, we can quickly become numb and calloused, because we "cannot respond to every need." On the other hand, it is disconcerting that current practice often removes the donor from direct involvement in the compassionate touch through personally meeting the need. In responding to a need far away we may feel absolved from interacting with needs at our doorstep.

Christ's example to us, as well as the example of the early church, is one of personal involvement in touching needs. This compassion is evident first in Christ's compassionate act of coming to earth to give His life as a ransom so that those who believe in Him might have eternal life. It is further exemplified in His ministry on earth and in the ministry of His followers. As they went about their daily activities, they would often stop out of compassion for the hurting and minister to them. Therefore, we, as individual believers, and the church corporately, should follow this example in our compassionate ministry. Since Christ's model of compassionate acts, and the precedence of the New Testament church, gives us a clear example of involvement in compassionate ministry, how then shall we move forward with the greatest effectiveness? Byron Klaus offers some helpful "guidelines for social concern":

- We must manifest the love of God and help, as we are able, those around us. God expects us to give productive manifestations of the love of God.
- The local church is the center of all ministry to social concern.
- We should be sure our ministry is reaching real needs. We should not enter into wasteful competition with secular agencies.
- We should minister so as to help people help themselves.
- We should remember only those things done for the redemption of humanity will stand for eternity.[30]

May it be that, as Pentecostals, our Spirit-empowered witness, coupled with Spirit-directed compassionate acts, will propel our testimony to greater visibility whereby the eternal, life-changing gospel will be proclaimed, and Christ's compassion will be known, through us and truly transform our society and our world in ways otherwise unattainable.

## MISSIONARY PRESENCE

With the present difficulty many missionaries are having raising their budgets, should compassion ministry take a back burner to a perceived greater priority of placing more missionaries on the field? Secondly, many new missionaries are going to do compassionate work, rather than being involved in training ministries. Will this emphasis lead to deficiencies in our foundational work of training?

## FUNDING PRIORITY

With the current appeal of compassion ministries and the huge training need on the continent of Africa, how can we balance the need for financing theological training with the overwhelming appeal of compassionate work?

Since both of these concerns relate to funding issues, I will address them together. First, if Hudson Taylor was right, the finance of any work that is directed and driven by the Spirit will not lack the financial resources to carry out the work.[31] Both missionaries and national churches need to have an abundance mentality, believing that God has enough resources to train future leaders for the church, but to also express Christ's love through compassionate acts to those in need. We all need to earnestly work and pray for this to become a reality. It is both/and, rather than either/or thinking.[32] Having said that, I know the realities under which we all operate. I know of no kingdom ministry that enjoys unlimited resources to develop all of the programs deserving their time energy and attention. So, how do we decide where to invest the resources God has given to our care?[33]

Perhaps the problem centers on our need for better expressing the need to the donor base. Largely, the West does not understand the African training model. They overlay their concept of theological training over the African grid, and assume it is further down the list in causes worthy of their support. By and large, US theological training programs do not give the impetus for church planting and growth, whereas in Africa our training programs are the hothouse seedbed of our church growth. Nor in the US is there the great host of untrained pastors that we find across Africa.

It seems there are some proactive steps that can be taken that will assist the church in Africa to channel funds to the areas of our greatest need. Those in leadership positions need to be vocal about asking donors to re-direct funds to the area where the greatest effect will be achieved. The place of greatest need and impact is not usually apparent to a donor who is thousands of miles removed. Further, the African church needs to give clear instructions on the proper way to effectively implement compassion ministry without creating dependency or destroying local initiative. One way this can be done is through local capacity building. On-the-way compassion focuses on the twin priorities of evangelism and training to give the needed support to a growing church but does not ignore human need as it is encountered.

In Africa today, with its swelling shortage of adequately trained pastors, we must remain focused on placing trained pastors in pulpits and preparing these pastors in such a way that they complement the vision of their host churches. With limited resources, there can be a perceived competition for funds between a huge priority need (trained pastors) and the continually pressing need of the poor and needy (Matt. 26:11). An additional layer to this tension is that funds coming from the West seem to be more and more focused on compassion ministries while our theological training programs lack many necessities to do their work effectively.

The Western church generally has an inadequate understanding of either the training need or its importance to the work our churches across Africa are diligently working to advance. This is further exacerbated by the constant images projected to the West of the compassionate needs across the Majority World. One no longer needs to be walking to the post office in some African city to be faced with a humanitarian need. They are faced with it on TV every evening on their living rooms. Further, this need is magnified many times over through amplified visuals from multiplied localities. This explains why a young pastor sitting in an Africa's Hope board meeting a few years ago gave a lengthy explanation as to why Africa's Hope should somehow repackage what we are doing as compassion ministry rather than training because "my people will give to compassion ministry."

The western church often sees theological education as being disconnected from the purpose for which it has been established. This disconnection is the natural tendency if not intentionally hedged against. Donors need to realize that in Africa we move intentionally to design each training program to fulfill a vital role in planting and growing the church. In some places the West has lost its understanding that to be fully effective, theological education must remain tied to the need in the local church. Further, compassionate ministries, as attractive as they may be to churches in the West, if not done skillfully, do not address root issues and can actually reduce local capacity rather than build it. Training is capacity building.

In her book, *From the Roots Up*, JoAnn Butrin points out that those interested in assisting with compassion ministry should not begin with what tugs at their heart out of the many needs that they may be aware of, but rather by asking the church in the country to which they feel compelled to give, what their greatest needs are. If they are set on addressing compassionate work, what is the best way to help, that is, what is sustainable and does not create dependency or subvert local initiative? She uses as an example the common desire of a church in the West to build an orphanage. She suggests that the receiving church say,

> "Well, we really don't want to do an orphanage for these reasons, but we think we have a better plan to help our orphans. And we believe there is a significant role that you can play." They might suggest, "Would you be will-

ing to come and build a group home?" Or, "Would you be willing to fund a small bakery so our kids could learn to bake bread, or so we could have an ongoing way to support the families that are taking in AIDS orphans, etc.?"[34]

After quoting John V. York and Ivan Satyavrata on "genuine and abiding friendships as partnerships," Butrin comments,

> Much has been written about the difficulties of maintaining true partnerships between *haves* and *haves not* entities, especially because it is usually the *haves* that come with and control the funding and thereby have the power. One could apply this to missionary/national relationships in many instances, as well. If one truly approaches these relationships as friendships, looking out for the good of each other, there may be a possibility of mutual trust developing more quickly.[35]

Butrin then goes on to offer some very helpful suggestions regarding dialogue between donor and recipient regarding need and expectations.[36]

Dambisa Moyo, Harvard graduate and economist, in her book, *Dead Aid*, points out in a compelling way how much of the aid Africa has received through the years has been counterproductive.[37] She shows how, in some instances, aid has undercut local initiative, lined the pockets of politicians, and has been designated to be spent in areas that were not of primary importance. Butrin points out that there are similar issues in church based initiatives:

> Buildings can be…a reminder and often embarrassment to those who are involved in plans gone awry. These would include multi-story buildings that were intended to be hospitals, orphanages, community centers, or factories. Their internal workings, however, were not figured into the budget or the plan of those who so enthusiastically constructed them. And so they sit, empty shells, often monuments to the egos of those who thought they knew best. They hadn't gone through the arduous and often time consuming steps of figuring out what's happening and what needs to happen along with the people who know. No thought was given to local ownership and things arising "from the roots up."[38]

All of this seems to tell us that we must do several things better. We need to communicate the need more effectively to the donor base in the West. This would include encouraging donors to re-direct funds to the areas that will produce the greatest effect for the kingdom of God. This means we need to promote a long-range strategy as opposed to a short-term outlook that seems to meet an immediate need but may ignore the long-range implications of addressing the immediate need. We need to offer compelling strategies that will address both the humanitarian need and the growth and vitality of the church, because these two are inextricably linked. This leads to the final area of consideration, delivery systems.

## DELIVERY SYSTEMS

How do we package compassion ministry on the continent? Should compassion ministry funding be coupled with theological training and/or evangelism efforts?

**Contextualized Training**

Because it is a common tendency of academics to raise many questions but offer few answers, let me now focus on potential solutions to the "theological tension" between compassionate ministries and theological training. Theological training provides a fitting venue to train future leaders in compassionate ministry which can be done in a number of creative ways. Some of these ways can mutually benefit the institution, the learner, and the compassionate ministry. The key is not to lock our training programs into predetermined patterns that do not fit our needs on the continent. The African church needs to continually evaluate its theological training programs in light of both financial realities and the training needs of the church. In the same way that we do not want the Western donor base to dictate financial priorities for African churches, we do not want Western forms of theological training to blindly dictate to us what our African training models should be.

The African church must ask itself, "Are our training programs based on western Enlightenment systems or on a more biblical model?" How was ministry formation done in Old Testament prophetic circles? What was Jesus' model in training His disciples? How did Paul mentor those whom he raised up for ministry? It seems that an examination of how ministry formation took place in biblical times can inform our current practice to greater effectiveness.

It is an area that is essentially unexplored in theological training today largely because the church is committed to its well-established educational intuitions, institutions that are struggling for survival in the West.[39]

The biblical model is much more hands on, more of a mentorship and/or apprenticeship approach. A more biblical model could be utilized effectively across Africa, especially at the lay- and diploma-levels of training. This would effectively close the gap between theory and practice, offering the learner greater opportunity to reflect on the subject, while also applying it in practical ways. This apprenticeship or "in-service-training" model would temper our current methods of theological education with a more holistic and practical element, thus increasing capacity for training without removing the learner from the local context. It would also speed the rate at which training can take place, which addresses a great need on the continent.

We currently have some outstanding examples of this kind of training by extension in a number of places in Africa, one of which is in Kenya. This kind of training allows for the implementation of more creative approaches to training that would be more in keeping with the real needs pastors face doing ministry in Africa. The training could involve students with micro-enterprise and/or compassion ministry as part of their training. This is already taking place in some schools on the continent.[40]

A biblical training approach could connect compassion ministry with theological training in new and creative ways in which the training program becomes the vehicle through which compassion ministry is both learned and expressed. Since compassion ministries should be connected to the church and church ministries, this provides another avenue through which this connection can be made. A contextualized approach that is designed to meet Africa's humanitarian needs and its development potential could greatly enhance our training programs.

In his reflection on Lausanne III, Allen Yeh pointed out the need for contextualized theological training:

> The Majority World already has more Christians than the Western World does. As such, except for areas of Unreached People Groups, what they are lacking is not evangelism, but resources and training. One of the most necessary missiological priorities today is to mobilize local Christians to minister in their own contexts. Bringing theological training without Western culture

is difficult without an understanding of contextualization, a topic which unfortunately was not touched upon much at the Congress.[41]

Focusing on a contextualized theological training model that addresses humanitarian and development needs as well as in-service training seems to me to be a viable answer to the missional tension that is perceived to exist between theological training and compassion ministries. The Commission on Accreditation and Endorsement, one of the three commissions of the newly established Association for Pentecostal Theological Education in Africa (APTEA), would do well to establish this as part of their evaluation of schools. They could address issues such as

- How effective is the institution in contextualizing its training approach?
- Are there practical in-service training programs that go beyond the ecclesiastical duties in preparing the student for addressing humanitarian and development needs?
- Have the faculty incorporated into their classroom instruction issues addressing social responsibility?
- Has the school considered incorporating some aspects of development training that could also be a source of income for the school and future ministers?
- Beyond educating the student, has the school considered training the students' spouses in tentmaking abilities that could also become a basis for community development?

**Faculty Development**

A second area that could be addressed relates to the area of faculty development. Is the classroom instruction going beyond a purely academic approach? Are the faculty members addressing practical real-life issues in and outside the classroom? Are the realities of the massive social needs that exist in society being addressed in the classroom? To effectively meet the needs of contemporary African society, Bible school instructors need to go beyond teaching content and knowledge only. The content and knowledge must be related to life in real and practical ways that will prepare the student for ministry in a desperately needy society. Robert Banks addresses this issue:

Alongside technical knowledge of their subject area, teachers require an intimate acquaintance with the One who is present in it and animates it. Our language is interesting here: we talk about "subjects" but often communicate them as objects. Only if teachers are in vital touch with the presence of God in their area of expertise, whatever that happens to be, will they be able to communicate this in a life-giving, life-changing, way. It is not just their competence to deal with the subject matter that counts, but the extent to which the subject personally matters to them! What we are talking about here is *passion*, though the expression of this will vary from one person to the next.[42]

If our theological education is going to be effective in training future ministers of the gospel, we must start with the trainers. As theological educators "we do not just *present* truth, we must *represent* it to others. We do not just relate the truth in the hope that others might comprehend it, we relate to them in a way that helps them begin to be apprehended by it."[43] The student's ability will seldom go beyond that of their professors. Not only must the faculty of our Bible schools teach on compassion, they must also model it to the student. It is personally gratifying to see the effect of the newly established "Teaching for Life" program. This program was established by Africa Theological Training Service, and now continues as the Commission on Faculty Development and Enrichment under APTEA. I believe this commission will continue to be fruitful in developing teachers who effectively develop life-changing leaders for the future of the church of Africa.

## A Biblical Theology of Compassion Ministry

A third area that could be addressed is the development of a biblical theology of compassion ministry. In my search for a theology of compassion ministry there was a dearth of material that addressed the subject from a biblically sound hermeneutical approach. Cheyne does a good job of addressing the major issues, but I would not call his work entirely a hermeneutical-theological approach. Late in my research I did find one book that effectively addressed the issues from more of what I would view as a hermeneutical-theological perspective.[44] Although I was not in total agreement with all it contained, it is a step in the right direction. This is a subject matter that is ripe with potential for the African writer to address from an African contextual perspective. The Western church desperately needs some direction from the

Majority World on how to address compassion and justice from the perspective of a biblically-based theological model.

This is something I would like to recommend to the APTEA Commission on Scholarly Writing. A thorough biblical theology of compassion ministry would address, not only biblical texts that address compassion and justice (which seems to be the norm in books on compassion ministry—somewhat of a topical approach), but also how these were practically addressed in the Old and New Testaments.

For some time our schools have been in need of a curriculum that addresses compassionate and humanitarian issues. Later this year, a Discovery Series textbook will be printed, called *Transformational Development and the Church*. This book will be a tremendous tool in the hands of our African trainers to begin to address compassionate ministry in the African context. Given the magnitude of the humanitarian crisis across Africa, this text should become a standard course for our schools. This course, coupled with some practical application in holistic ministry, is a step in the right direction.

ENDNOTES

[1] David J. Bosch, *Transforming Mission: Paradigm Shifts in Theology of Mission* (Maryknoll, NY: Orbis, 1991), 401.

[2] http://www.lausanne.org/covenant

[3] John R. Cheyne, *Incarnational Agents: A Guide to Developmental Ministry* (Birmingham, AL: New Hope, 1996), 23. (Digital copy, the page number may be different in the printed copy.)

[4] http://wwwlusanne.org/all-documents/lop-21.html, Introduction

[5] Ibid.

[6] Ibid.

[7] Ibid., 23

[8] "Compassion Statement," Assemblies of God World Missions, Executive Committee, 2003.

[9] Ibid.

[10] A sideline concern that I have is that the AG/USA does a lot of its compassion ministry through Convoy of Hope. After the Katrina hurricane crisis in the US a few years ago I took note of a newspaper article that listed organizations that came to the assistance of the region and the amount of help that was given in dollars. Many mainline and evangelical denominations were listed. The Assemblies

of God was absent from the list; however, Convoy of Hope was listed. The unfortunate reality is that the typical reader would not be aware that the AG sent its compassion funds through Convoy of Hope. Therefore, it appears that the AG is not involved in compassionate concerns. One might respond that we do not do it for the recognition, which is true. However, perception is reality and it gives the appearance that the AG just does not care.

[11] Byron Klaus "Compassion Rooted in the Gospel That Transforms" PowerPoint.

[12] As quoted by Pius Tembu, General Secretary of the Kenya Assemblies of God, at the founding meetings of APTEA, February 2011.

[13] Jamie Gates and Jon Middendorf, *Living Justice: A Revolutionary Compassion in A Broken World* (Kansas City, MO: Barefoot Ministries, 2007), 30-31.

[14] Cheyne, 24.

[15] It is interesting to note that some US churches are renaming their missions departments by removing the name "missions" and replacing it with the word "compassion." I recently received an e-mail from a church that the title of the person sending the email was "Compassions Manager." A recent article by Colin Andrews in the June, 2011, *Evangelical Missions Quarterly* entitled, "The Death of Missions: An EMQ Symposium," highlights this trend (http://www.emisdirect.com/emq/issue ]315/2533, accessed April 1, 2011).

[16] JoAnn Butrin, *From the Roots Up: A Closer Look at Compassion and Justice in Missions* (n.c.: Roots Up Publishers, 2010), 172-173.

[17] Klaus, PowerPoint.

[18] Jeff Nelson, "Integral Mission and Developmental Challenges Among the Rendille People of Kenya: Association Pentecostal Perspective." Research paper submitted to Dr. Enson Lwesya, Pan-Africa Theological Seminary, June 2010, 28-29.

[19] Ibid., 8.

[20] Bryant L. Myers, *Walking with the Pour: Principles and Practices of Transformational Development* ( Maryknoll, NY: Orbis, 1999 and 2006), 35.

[21] Bryan P. Stone, *Compassionate Ministry: Theological Foundations* (Marynoll, NY: Orbis, 2004), 10.

[22] Ibid., 13.

[23] Ibid., 17.

[24] Ibid., 19.

[25] Baptizing and teaching are equally important in making disciples. In the Greek, "make disciples" is an imperative. "Baptizing" and "teaching" are partici-

ples that give content to what it means to make disciples. Therefore, our work is not done once a person is brought to a confession of faith. For more, see Donald McGavran, *The Bridges of God: A Study in the Strategy of Mission* (NY: Friendship Press, 1955), 13-16. See also Ronald Sider, *Good News and Good Works*, 76-79, where he outlines seven differences we must understand if the gospel is more than just forgiveness of sins.

[26] As is stated in the Lausanne documents, evangelism is primary which seems to be in keeping with the message of God's word.

[27] Howard Snyder, *Liberating the Church* (Downers Grove, IL: InterVarsity, 1983), 161-162.

[28] Because of time and space I have mainly focused on the New Testament example. For a brief overview of Old Testament patterns (see Appendix 6).

[29] Of course this would not apply to natural disasters where the church can, and should, respond in the love of Christ to an immediate and critical need as they are able. However, in our response, care must be taken not to allow the current critical need to create a state of dependency, rather to provide a means by which those in need can be enabled to remedy their own situation. Ideally, in these crisis situations, it would be best for the church to respond first to those in the household of faith, then beyond that to all those in need.

[30] Klaus, PowerPoint.

[31] "God's work done in God's way never will lack God's supply."

[32] James C. Collins and Jerry I. Porras, *Built to Last* (New York, NY: Harper Business, 1994).

[33] For a good discussion of balancing evangelistic efforts with compassion ministry see Ronald Sider, *Good News and Good Works,* 165-171, where he addresses five questions of primacy.

[34] Butrin, 115-116.

[35] Ibid., 129.

[36] Ibid., 130ff.

[37] Dambisa Moyo, *Dead Aid: Why Aid Is Not Working and How Three Is a Better Way for Africa* (New York, NY: Farrar, Straus and Giroux, 2009).

[38] Butrin, 147-148.

[39] As evidenced by the recent proposal for a merger between Evangel University, Central Bible College, and the Assemblies of God Theological Seminary.

[40] Burkina Faso has students involved in agriculture and weaving. A school in Togo trains students' wives in sewing as well as English skills. These kinds of programs can serve as models for theological training programs in other countries.

⁴¹ Allen Yeh, "A Participants Account of Lausanne III" (Evangelical Missions Quarterly, January 2011) (http://www.emisdirect.com/emq/issue-314/2502, accessed March 10, 2011).

⁴² Robert Banks, *Re-envisioning Theological Education: Exploring a Missional Alternative to Current Model* (Grand Rapids, MI: Eerdmans, 1999), 175.

⁴³ Ibid., 174.

⁴⁴ Ronald, J. Sider, *Good News and Good Works* (Grand Rapids: Baker, 1993). Sider gives a thoughtful, well researched, and extremely well-documented theology of compassion ministry. He begins with outlining four common models while pointing out their deficiencies. He then dedicates the remainder of the book to offering a fifth model and giving the theological underpinnings of this model.

# Missional Tensions in Africa: A Response to the Paper by William Kirsch

DOUGLAS LOWENBERG

In this review, I will summarize the salient thoughts articulated by Dr. Bill Kirsch in his paper on "Missional Tension," develop a conversation between Kirsch and others concerning some of the significant issues, and conclude with a few personal reflections on this timely, tension-laden topic. While Kirsch discusses the place of compassionate ministries within the ministerial training curricula of our Bible schools and seminaries in Africa, his major attention is given to the tension that exists on a much wider scale between evangelism and ministries of compassion. His article attempts to resolve the tension between these two seemingly exclusive ministries, or propose a beneficial synergy between evangelism and compassion, by developing a biblical theology of compassion ministries which Kirsch himself states is "the main focus of this paper." His second emphasis is the need for and the present status of missional workers engaged in Bible school (theological) training and those doing compassion ministries. Thirdly, he considers the sufficiency of financial resources from the Western world, especially the Assemblies of God (USA), to assist with the pressing needs of both spheres in terms of supporting Bible school personnel and sponsoring compassionate ministry projects. Fourthly, Kirsch proposes strategies for integrating training for compassionate ministries into the academic and practical curricula of our Bible schools.

BRIEF SUMMARY

## A Biblical Theology of Compassion Ministries

To develop a biblical theology of compassion ministries, Kirsch rightly states that the focus for such a task must be on Holy Scripture. As texts are investigated, the exegete must search for the biblical author's inspired intention for writing the passage and the meaning the text had for its first audience. As the meaning and intention of the passage is interpreted for the contemporary audience, the inspired message that God wanted communicated to a particular audience in real time and history must be made relevant to our historical, cultural, material, and spiritual context without dilution, deletion, or addition. A collation of texts leads to the development of a theology which in turn must then be fleshed out in practices that are pleasing to God and consistent with the meaning of actions described in Scripture.

Kirsch's biblical theology of compassion ministries is anchored on three texts from the Gospel of Matthew: 25:31-46 (especially verse 40), the parable of the sheep and the goats; 22:37-40, the Great Commandments, love God and love your neighbor; and 28:18-20, the Great Commission to make disciples of all the nations (μαθητεύσατε πάντα τά ἔθνη).[1] Kirsch affirms the conclusion of the authors of the Lausanne document who said, "Matthew 25 speaks to the fact that we will be judged according to the depth of our compassion for human need." He sees the need for a both/and understanding of loving God with all that a person is and loving her neighbor as herself: "Both are primary and they are to be held in balance." With a unique synthesis, he combines the Great Commandments with the Great Commission to formulate the following: "Because of your love for Me, go to the nations and make disciples by baptizing them, and teaching them to obey my commands, and as you go, love them as you do yourself."

He explains that who we are, our manner, our identity, our DNA, is founded on the Great Commandment: we are "lovers of God and of people." Our compassion is a byproduct of Christ's compassion and flows from our being. We demonstrate the love of Christ in our unconditional love for others. On the other hand, our mission, our method, the Great Commission, is to reach the lost by transmitting the gospel message and making disciples through training. If I correctly understand Kirsch, compassion is who we are; mission is what we do.

The two aspects of manner and mission, who we are and what we do, Great Commandments and Great Commission, happen simultaneously through what Kirsch describes as "compassion on the way." As we go about reaching the lost, we respond with compassion to human need. While journeying to reach the unreached, we take side trips to touch those needing compassion.

Kirsch's biblical theology of compassion ministries requires the personal involvement of Christians in acts of compassion as opposed to giving to a need from a safe distance. Rather than hypocritical, distant, sanitized giving, individual, congregational and corporate donors should have direct, relational contact with those needing expressions of holistic compassion. He declares, "The church must teach the difference between having compassion and giving funds for the poor."

## Workers Engaged in Theological Training and in Compassion Ministries

Quoting an oft repeated statement of our AGWM African regional director, Mike McClaflin, Kirsch writes, "If all our missionaries were forced to leave Africa, the last one out would be a Bible school trainer." Kirsch, along with his readers, struggles to reconcile this priority with the reality that the Assemblies of God (USA) in recent years has placed a greater focus on compassionate ministries than the theological training of African pastors. He refers to JoAnn Butrin, AGWM Regional Director of compassionate ministries, who insinuates that is not politically correct to question the holistic and humanitarian initiatives of the Assemblies of God and AGWM.

Doing a quick calculation of our AGWM missionary personnel in Kenya, of 17 family units, four are involved full-time in pastoral training ministries at our Bible college/university and seminary. AGWM has no full-time personnel teaching at Addis Ababa Bible College or the Assemblies of God Bible College (Dodoma, TZ). The West Africa Advanced School of Theology, Lomé, Togo, at one time had at least eight families teaching full-time. Presently there are two. While it is difficult to clearly define missionary job descriptions and assignments, and while overlap is abundant, it is clear that the numbers serving in training ministries has diminished while those participating in compassion ministries have grown significantly. McClaflin may have to reconsider his proverb: If all the missionaries were forced to leave Africa, the Bible school trainers have already exited.

Fortunately, God has raised up a host of capable and gifted African teachers who are providing instruction in our Bible schools across the continent. With or without the partnership of teachers from other nations, theological training is moving forward at an accelerated pace. However, indigenous compassionate ministries seem more dependent on foreign personnel and funding than theological training.

## Adequacy of Finances to Sustain Theological Training and Ministries of Compassion

Kirsch references Hudson Taylor, mid-nineteenth century missionary to China and founder of the China Inland Mission, who said that God's will, done in God's way, will not lack God's provision. Kirsch claims there are abundant resources in the West that can support both pastoral training and ministries of compassion in terms of personnel and ministries. But funds are limited and unable to address all the educational and humanitarian needs on the continent. The article rightly admonishes us to have an abundance mentality and not be competitive or jealous over donations to either compassion or training ministries, or those who facilitate these ministries.[2] Kirsch is correct that in the AG (USA) there is a misunderstanding of the method and purpose of training in Africa. Better communication of the purpose of Bible school and seminary training and the profound impact her graduates are having in Africa must be articulated.

He recommends that Bible schools in Africa which integrate theological and compassion training in their curricula appeal for funding from the West that then can simultaneously assist both training and compassion. Synthesizing the Great Commandments and Great Commission in our Bible schools may appeal to donors who have overlooked the viability and long-term impact trained, indigenous, culturally-sensitive pastors can have both on the church and their social and economic environment.

Kirsch mentions the donor-drivenness that impacts strategies and initiatives both for AGWM administration and local personnel, as well as national church leaders and pastors. More often than not, those coming with the finances dictate where and how the money will be spent. Donors give according to their perspectives, burdens, and emotions, which do not always mesh with national church priorities. While Western funds at this juncture in history continue to flow to Africa, the cultural bent of the Westerner to respond to felt need typically results in giving to compassion ministries where they see vivid images of homelessness, hunger, and disease.

Later in this review more will be said about the potential for indigenous financial support of compassion ministries. Both the mission and the national church must consciously avoid repeating the mistake made in early Evangelical and Pentecostal missions where cross-cultural ministries, especially with the target being the unreached people groups, were relegated to the mission only. Just as national churches and mission personnel together must participate in apostolic function in terms of evangelizing and discipling the unreached people groups of Africa, donations for and participation in compassion ministries must come from both sources.[3]

## Integrating Training for Compassion Ministries into the Bible School Curriculum

A solution to the tension between theological training and compassion ministries is to offer both in our schools. Kirsch recommends that academic communities embrace compassion, training their students in compassion ministries, which can heighten the effectiveness of local churches in reaching and touching their communities. Bible teachers need to develop their biblical theology of compassion, become more informed of different avenues of compassionate ministry, and promote them in their classes. Through the local church, humanitarian need can be alleviated. Students need training, not only in theology and pastoral duties, but in developing a capacity to respond to human, physical, and tangible need. "We should look at compassionate ministries and theological training as a unified whole." Kirsch proposes that this type of training will best happen through in-service delivery systems where students come to our schools for limited periods of time so they can stay fully engaged in the local church context, receive hands-on experiences of touching the poor, learn about micro-enterprising and platforms for tentmaking, and blend the theoretical and practical. While biblical instructors need to become more informed about compassion ministries, workers of compassion need to bring their skills to the Bible school classroom to participate in the training process.

## CONVERSATIONS WITH A LARGER AUDIENCE REGARDING MISSIONAL TENSION

In this section of the review, the dialogue will be expanded to include the perspectives of several authors regarding the four major subjects highlighted in the summary.

**A Biblical Theology of Compassion Ministries**

While the Lausanne Committee has helped to integrate evangelism and compassion ministries, reducing the chasm and tension between the two, not all would agree with their interpretation of Matthew 25:40 regarding the giving of a cup of cold water in His name to the least of these. Most interpreters agree that the "least" could be anyone experiencing poverty and oppression, Christians in general who are suffering, or apostolic representatives of Jesus who travel to resistant regions to proclaim the gospel and suffer because of their mission. Joe Kapolyo's conclusion is that one need not to choose between the three. "We are called to respond to all human need for that is what love does."[4]

D. A. Carson differs with Kapolyo. He states, "As people respond to his disciples, or 'brothers,' and align themselves with their distress and afflictions, they align themselves with the Messiah who identifies himself with them (v. 45). True disciples will love one another and serve the least brother with compassion.... We must not think that the Bible is unconcerned for the poor and the oppressed (Deut. 15:11; Matt. 22:37-40; 26:11; Gal. 2:10). But that is not the center of interest here."[5] It seems that Matthew emphasized Jesus' parable to encourage indigenous missionaries, not the Paul's and Peters and Apolloses, to fulfill their calling to faithfully proclaim the gospel to the nations, whether receptive or resistant, because the nation's response determined their eternal destiny.

Craig Keener adds additional perspective to Matthew's Gospel as he reports that the book contains a "sizeable body of material in favor of the Gentile mission."[6] It is possible, though uncertain, that Matthew wrote to the Church in Antioch consisting of Jews and Gentiles (Acts 11:19-21). Adding to the cultural and religious segregation between Jews and Gentiles, the massacre of Jews by Roman legions between AD 66-70 would have deepened the rift and prejudice between the two.[7] Early Christian missionaries would have encountered hostilities from Jews and Gentiles and experienced hunger, thirst, homelessness, nakedness, sickness, and imprisonment. They were to endure hardship, like their Lord, realizing that individuals and nations would be judged according to how they responded to the gospel and its messengers. "One treats Jesus as one treats his representatives."[8] My conclusion: this text does not serve as a proof text for compassion ministries to any and all who are in need.

Miriam Smith, missionary to Kenya, calls for a holistic approach to missions that includes word-deed-and sign.[9] She writes,

> [Evangelism] means sharing the good news with my whole life; my words, my deeds and with signs and wonders. My word is not the only witness; it is also my lifestyle, my loving actions, my sacrifice for others, and the power of the Holy Spirit working through me as a sign of God's presence and power."[10]

John V. York wrote, "We know where God's mission is heading by looking at how it concludes. There will be 'a great multitude that no one [can] count, from every nation, tribe, people and language' (Rev. 7:9)."[11] He added,

> Missionaries must never lose sight of Christ's declaration, "I will build my church" (Matt. 16:18). It is my position that this is a controlling statement when it comes to mission strategy. Building the Church is the immediate object of mission. From the Church, as it is built, the ministries of Christ are extended to the world.... The starting place for missions, then, is simply the extension of the local church—throughout its immediate environment and onward throughout the entire earth.... To fail to have a plan for opening new churches, or cells of believers, is to signal betrayal of the mission of God.[12]

While, for Kirsch, responding to human need with acts of compassion comes from who we are rather than what we do, York places "compassion and human need" as a category under the larger heading of mission.[13] York calls the church to respond to human suffering with the goals of bringing significant change to the health conditions in local communities and planting churches, transforming people from without and within.

Kirsch's placement of "compassion on the way" as a natural and spontaneous response to human need as it is encountered in the process of evangelism agrees with the manner by which both Jesus and the early church responded to needy situations. On the way to the cross He responded with compassion to the spiritual and physical plight of those around Him. However, Jesus operated with the priority of seeing people willingly acknowledge His Lordship and enter into His spiritual kingdom, the kingdom of God, which was not of this world.[14] On the way to the cross, He did not have time to dialogue with inquiring Greek proselytes.[15] On the way to giving His flesh as the bread of life, He did not provide additional loaves of bread to satisfy the hunger of the unbelieving crowd.[16] On the way to manifesting Himself to be equal with God, He stopped at the Pool of Bethesda and healed one invalid while leaving a great multitude in their misery.[17] Further, Jesus' compassion on the way was marked by supernatural signs (multiplication of fish and bread, healings of disease and sickness, and deliverance from demonization) rather than our physical responses of distributing food, digging wells, building reservoirs, constructing churches and group homes, distributing medicines, and planting moringa trees.

The early church followed Jesus' example of word, deed, and sign but also alleviated suffering with non-supernatural, voluntary, sacrificial donations dispersed by Spirit-filled, honest elders primarily to believers.[18] Compassion ministries were not allowed to cause a neglect of the ministry of the word of God. A group of qualified individuals, distinct from the apostles who ministered the word, were selected to manage the distribution. As a result "the number of disciples increased rapidly" (Acts 6:7)[19] It is noteworthy that generous contributions from believers that were laid at the apostles' feet were distributed to anyone in need so that there was no needy person among them.[20] And apparently none of these funds made their way into the pockets of the apostles who confessed, "Silver and gold I do not have, but what I have I give you" (3:9)[21]

One significant difference between Kirsch's compassion theology and that of the early church is his encouragement of personal, direct involvement in touching human need. While trustworthy representatives carried finances from the haves to the have-nots, today's postmoderns want their own personal experience, wanting to see and touch for themselves.[22] Many Westerners today function with the postmodern worldview that is experiential, participatory and image-driven.[23] With these inner values and disposable funds to enable them to see and touch the needy, in the process of short-term, direct involvement, significant resources are consumed that could be used to alleviate more needs through the people already on the ground. However, this trend will continue, so it is better to work with those who come to see and touch so that they truly grasp the depth of the need and the necessity of sustainability in ministries that can bring lasting transformation and prepare people for eternity.

## The Workers Engaged in Theological Training and in Compassion Ministries

The need for laborers in the unharvested fields is great.[24] Whether they come from abroad or are local teachers for our schools who equip those who serve the church and society, they are needed. York righty says, "National churches want missionaries to do what they are not yet able to do."[25] There remains a great need for missionary teachers and missionary compassion facilitators to follow the Holy Spirit's leading and serve the expansion of God's kingdom with apostolic function. Those who have the ability to multi-task through training and serving should prioritize their time and do both. Donors need to be informed and encouraged to support both dimensions of ministry. A team, non-competitive mentality must govern the operation of our schools and compassion projects so that churches are planted and matured, and bring transformation to their communities' spirits, minds, emotions, and bodies.

## Adequacy of Finances to Sustain Theological Training and Ministries of Compassion

While a holistic approach to gospel ministry requires a response to the spiritual and physical needs of people, the latter aspect, which is more observable and seemingly more urgent, does generate larger contributions than evangelism and church-planting efforts that do not include a compassionate dimension. C. Gordon Olson expresses concern: "While meeting a very real need, development projects always have the serious danger of diverting missionary resources from their primary purpose—evangelism. Indeed, so frequently has evangelism gotten lost or repressed in these projects that serious consideration must constantly be given to maintaining it"[26] (see Appendix 8).

Alan Johnson expresses concern that the proliferation of activity from our western Christians threatens to choke the ability of the church to take the gospel to the 40% of the world's population who are least-reached and unreached.[27] There is the perception that everything a church does is missions and every Christian is a missionary. Further, everything the church does that helps people and improves their plight is of equal importance. These assumptions need to be challenged and evaluated through the lens of apostolic function.

Because the western mind is deeply influenced by postmodernism, the younger generations will have the tendency to give to the images they see and feel. As Leonard Sweet reports that the postmodern worldview is image-driven rather than word-based.[28] Pictures, images, and media influence their thoughts, actions, and contributions more than the literary and verbal content conveyed through a book, speech, or sermon.

Our current global economic realities are affecting the amount of disposable income available to many families in the West. While their tithe may be sustained, additional contributions may decrease. And while it is important to maintain an "abundance mentality," missional and indigenous ministries should admit that funding from external sources is not limitless. However, a growing donor base that has not been tapped as it should is African-generated resources. The African church, its leadership, and the Christian business community, as growing affluence is experienced, must be challenged to contribute to compassion and theological training initiatives. Even the poor can give as the church in Macedonia who in extreme poverty responded with rich generosity.[29] A robust indigenous church will be self-assisting with compassion just as it is self-leading, self-evangelizing, and self-supporting.

**Integrating Training for Compassion Ministries into the Bible School Curriculum**

National church leadership in conjunction with local Bible school administration and faculty need to reevaluate the mission statements of their schools in light of holistic missional ministry. If their theological perspective has the three-fold perspective identified by Johnson, then their training curriculum should reflect these values and must equip students to reach the unreached people groups with the gospel and plant the church where it has not been before, to plant and strengthen churches among those people groups where the church already exists, and to participate in ministries of compassion that alleviate suffering, promote justice, and pursue healthy, wholesome living. To accomplish these purposes, changes in courses, textbooks, and faculty may be needed.

These changes must be guided by the vision and the mission of the school which should be based on the mission of God (*missio Dei*). Africa's Bible school leadership teams will have to withstand influences from foreign and local donors, western philosophies and methods of education, and African federal commissions of higher education that attempt to highjack the schools for the purposes of their own agendas.

## CONCLUDING WITH PERSONAL REFLECTIONS

We, especially those of us from the West, have created many false dichotomies that need correction. A few might be the distinction between faith and works, words and deeds, being and doing, love of God and love of others, love of others and love of self, the physical and spiritual, the natural world and the spirit world.[30] Who we are cannot be divided from what we do. Since love must express itself as action generated from the One who fills our lives, we love God and people; we witness of Christ to those around us; we serve people, especially the needy ones in the Kingdom; and we obey the Holy Spirit's command to go and reach the unreached. However, some bifurcations are significant. Healing through miraculous encounters and through medical assistance are healings accomplished by God's grace, but they are different in the source of power. Alleviating suffering in a physical body and removing unjust systems that impose bondage and oppression are not the same as seeing a person cleansed from the ravages of sin and delivered from the enslaving powers of Satan and demons through the name of Jesus. While we must care for and love people as whole persons (body, soul, and spirit) with our entire beings, we realize the temporality of this life and body; they are not made for eternity.

Jesus came to deal with eternal issues but on the way He expressed compassion through miraculous interventions. At His birth the angelic messenger said His name was to be Jesus because He will save His people from their sins.[31] He came to seek and save what was lost.[32] He said He came to earth for a specific reason which He had to embrace, His death on the cross.[33] He said that this gospel of the kingdom will be preached in the whole world as a testimony to all nations, and then the end will come.[34] He commanded His followers of all ages to make disciples of the nations by going, baptizing, and teaching.[35] From conception to glorification as King of kings and Lord of lords, His primary mission is reconciling sinners to God, empowering them to live righteously in this life, and preparing them for their eternal destination.

No matter our geographical or cultural location or our ministry, our ultimate purpose and mission must align with His: love people, which means wanting and doing what is best for them no matter the cost and without expectations of compensation. The greatest act of love is to prepare them to meet God and be freed from enslaving sin. Secondly, my love causes me to try to improve their quality of life individually and systemically. It is a both/and.

We accept the reality that neither Jesus, nor the early church, nor we will heal everyone in this life and alleviate all injustice and oppression. The making of all things new awaits the eschaton. We must remember that people who have believed in Jesus as their Lord and Savior will enter into heaven and experience instant and complete healing from their crippled emaciated bodies, leaving behind social settings of corruption, oppression, and injustice to bask in the life, peace, and wholeness of God's renewing presence. Willful sinners, independent of their physical condition, who suppress the truth that they have received will experience God's wrath for eternity.[36] Meanwhile, led by the Spirit, we proclaim the gospel to as many as we can through words, deeds, and signs, through a life poured out in service and compassion, learning language, living among the lost and the poor, confronting systems of evil and injustice so that the King and His kingdom may become resident among every people group.

Our priority missional activity is apostolic function, bringing the good news of the kingdom to peoples yet unreached in order to establish churches that will become self-leading, self-supporting, self-evangelizing (among their own people and language group), self-sending (to people groups different from themselves), self-theologizing (making the gospel, worship, and expressions of faith culturally relevant while biblically consistent), and self-assisting (believing communities sharing with the poor and needy among them with priority on believers). Africa's Christian leaders along with missionaries must work to establish the church in partnership, participating in all aspects of the life of the church as long as this partnership does not hinder the advance of the gospel to the regions beyond or the maturing of the indigenous saints.

AGWM has four pillars: reaching with evangelism, planting by establishing new churches, touching with ministries of compassion, and teaching in order to make disciples and prepare servant leaders to minister to God's church. What must bring the four pillars together?

They are linked through apostolic function. Alan Johnson observes three streams of missions: planting and growing churches in regions and among people groups where other churches already exist, expressing Christian social concern for the needy, and focusing on getting the gospel to unreached people groups where no church movement currently exists.[37] He admonishes all missionaries to meld the three paradigms as we participate in the fulfillment of the Great Commission.

The Brackenhurst Manifesto that emerged from a regional meeting of AGWM personnel in the East Africa-Indian Ocean Basin, clarified the commitment of these missionaries to eight core values: (1) abiding in Christ, (2) serving from the paradigm of apostolic function, (3) pioneering, (3) partnering, (5) living together as teams, (6) being life-long learners, (7) transforming people holistically in body, mind and spirit, and (8) living Pentecostally.[38] These core values are being implemented in a new initiative in East Africa called "Live Dead" where the vision is to see an indigenous church planted among all the unreached peoples of East Africa by teams of AGWM missionaries using means of creative access to engage the lost.[39]

The church and her training institutions will dispel missional tension as they respond sacrificially and holistically to Christ's final command by offering her people and resources to transform the human and spiritual conditions of those they encounter along the way to reaching the unreached with the good news of the Lordship of Christ and His kingdom which is already but not yet.

## ENDNOTES

[1] While Kirsch cites numerous biblical references throughout his article, these three seem most foundational for the development of his biblical theology of compassion ministries.

[2] Stephen R. Covey, in *Principle-Centered Leadership* (New York, NY: Simon & Schuster, 1992), 44-45, states that an abundance mentality "thinks win/win." Rather than being insecure and, because resources are scarce, grabbing all she can while she can, Covey says one must recognize her own worth, acknowledge the equal worthiness of others, believe that there is an abundance of resources to meet each need, and desire the mutual benefit of all people and ministries.

[3] For a full development of the meaning of apostolic function, see Alan R. Johnson, *Apostolic Function in $21^{st}$ Century Missions* (Springfield, MO: AGTS, 2009), 66-72. Apostolic function is a lens through which missionaries see themselves and conceive of both their identity and task. Functioning as apostles, they are committed to the proclamation of the gospel and the founding and administering of new churches among all the people groups of the world especially in those regions where there are no Christians or existing churches.

[4] Joe Kapolyo, "Matthew," in *Africa Bible Commentary* (Tokunboh Adeyemo, ed.; Nairobi: Word Alive, 2006), 1164.

[5] D. A. Carson. *Matthew* (EBC; Grand Rapids, MI: Zondervan, 1995), 522.

[6] Craig S. Keener, *Matthew* (IVPNTCS; Downers Grove, IL: InterVarsity, 1997 ), 29.

[7] Ibid., 33. The earliest manuscripts of Matthew were found in Antioch leading some to conjecture that Matthew wrote his gospel to the believers there to strengthen their faith in Jesus as Messiah and compel them to carry the message across all cultural, geographic, and ethnic barriers in order to make disciples of all nations. Antioch was the first great missionary church (Acts 13:1-3).

[8] Ibid., 361.

[9] Bryant L. Myers, *Walking with the Poor: Principles and Practices of Transformational Development* (Maryknoll, NY: Orbis, 2006) uses the same paradigm: word-deed-sign.

[10] Miriam Smith, "Holistic Worldview and Witness" (article presented to the Brackenhurst Manifesto Advisory Committee, Nairobi, Kenya, October 4, 2010), 13.

[11] John V. York, *Missions in the Age of the Spirit* (Springfield, Mo.: Logion, 2000), 239.

[12] Ibid., 240.

[13] Ibid., 246-7.

[14] John 18:36

[15] John 12:20-27

[16] John 6:25-66

[17] John 5:1-18

[18] For example, see Acts 2:44-47; 4:32-35; 6:1-7; 11:29-30; 2 Cor. 8:1-15; Gal. 6:10

[19] Acts 6:2, 4, 7

[20] Acts 4:34-35

[21] Acts 3:6

[22] See Acts 11:30; 2 Cor. 8:16-21

[23] Leonard Sweet, *Post-Modern Pilgrims: First Century Passion for the 21st Century Church* (Nashville, TN: Broadman and Holman Publishers, 2000.

[24] Matt. 9:37-38

[25] York, 243.

[26] C. Gordon Olson, *What in the World is God Doing?*, 4th ed. (Cedar Knolls, NJ: Global Gospel Publishers, 1998), 336.

[27] Johnson, *Apostolic Function*, 13. He reports that 40% of the world's population has either limited or no near-neighbor witness of the gospel.

[28] Sweet.

[29] 2 Cor. 8:2

[30] Johnson, 66, comments, "It is a telling sign of our tendency in the West to split the 'spiritual' and 'physical/social' domains that our images of apostolic ministry rarely include images of caring for the weak and marginalized." Some of the dichotomies have historical, theological causes such as the early twentieth-century swing in western theology to proclaiming a social gospel, rejecting the inspiration of the Word of God, and appealing for a moratorium on evangelistic missional activities. This topic is beyond the scope of this review. For further reading see Edgar J. Elliston, ed., *Christian Relief and Development: Developing Workers for Effective Ministry* (Dallas, TX: Word, 1989).

[31] Matt. 1:21

[32] Luke 19:10

[33] John 12:27-28

[34] Matt. 24:14

[35] Matt. 28:19-20
[36] Rom. 1:18-20; 2:5
[37] Johnson, 8.
[38] Dick Brogden and Greg Beggs, eds. "Brackenhurst Manifesto" (document drafted at the East Africa-Indian Ocean Basin Strategic Missions Meeting, Brackenhurst, Kenya, 2-7 January 2011).
[39] Greg Beggs, "Live Dead: Vision Strategy" paper (Nairobi, April 20, 2011).

## Appendix 1
## Resolution Calling for a "Decade of Pentecost"

[Adopted by the Africa Assemblies of God Alliance at its General Assembly on 5 March 2009 in Johannesburg, South Africa]

WHEREAS the Africa Assemblies of God Alliance has gone on record committing itself to missions involvement in the power of the Holy Spirit; and

WHEREAS AAGA has demonstrated that commitment by creating the World Missions Commission to inspire, facilitate, and coordinate missions involvement (2000) and the Acts in Africa Initiative to inspire and promote Pentecostal revival across the continent (2004); and

WHEREAS our churches across Africa stand ready to experience a fresh wind of the Spirit with millions of our members being baptized in the Holy Spirit and readied for missions involvement;

BE IT RESOLVED THAT the Africa Assemblies of God Alliance declare the coming decade (2010-2020) to be the "Decade of Pentecost."

BE IT FURTHER RESOLVED THAT during the Decade of Pentecost AAGA will call on its constituent national churches to promote a Pentecostal awakening in their churches aimed at empowering the church for greater evangelistic, missionary, and church planting involvement; and

BE IT FURTHER RESOLVED THAT Pentecost Sunday (the seventh Sunday following Easter) be declared "Pentecost Day" in each of our 50,000 (and growing)[1] churches across Africa, and that every pastor be encouraged to preach a message on the baptism in the Holy Spirit and missions on that day followed by prayer to receive the Spirit.

BE IT FURTHER RESOLVED THAT the Assemblies of God in Africa set as its goal to see 10 million of our members baptized in the Holy Spirit during the Decade of Pentecost.

Respectfully Submitted,
Dr. Denny Miller
Director
Acts in Africa Initiative

---

[1] At the time of the printing of this book the number of churches in the AG Africa has grown to 65,000.

# Appendix 2
# Vision 5:9 Fast Facts
# December 2010

**Currently there are**

- 2,221 MUPGs in which we seek effective church planting by 2025.
- 214 MUPGs with at least 100,000 in population are left to be engaged by 2012.

**Muslim Unreached People Groups Summary**

|  | Aug 2010 | Dec 2010 |
|---|---|---|
| Muslim Unreached People Groups | 2,227 | 2,221 |
| MUPGs equal to or greater than 100,000 | 703 | 699 |
| Unengaged | 214 | 214 |
| Engaged | 489 | 485 |
| Unknown | 0 | 0 |
| MUPGs less than 100,000 | 1,524 | 1,522 |
| Unengaged | 1,187 | 1,189 |
| Engaged | 337 | 333 |
| Unknown | 0 | 0 |

**Definitions**

*Affinity Bloc:* A large grouping of peoples related by language, history, and culture, and usually indigenous to a geographical location.

*People Cluster:* A smaller grouping of peoples within an affinity bloc, often with a common name or identity, but separated from one another by political boundaries, language, or migration patterns.

*People Group:* A smaller grouping of peoples within a people cluster of individuals who perceive themselves to have a common identity.

*Engagement:* We consider a Muslim People group effectively engaged when all four of the following elements are in place. There is

1. a pioneering church-planting effort in residence.
2. a commitment to work in the local language and culture.
3. a commitment to long-term ministry.
4. sowing in a manner consistent with the goal of seeing a church-planting movement (CPM) emerge.

# Appendix 3
# LATIN AMERICAN STATEMENT ON COOPERATION
## How We Relate to One Another Through Networking

CONSIDERING that the church of Christ is one, but is a diversity of members and that much is talked about in church circles about cooperation and unity on a Latin American scale, We must participate in a biblical unity that gives testimony to the world (John 17) but leaves in liberty the many members (1 Cor. 12:12) and respond to the call of our Lord without losing our identity and Pentecostal missionary philosophy.

What cooperation DOES NOT mean to us:

1. It does not mean a single world administrative organization.
2. It does not mean a single Latin America Assemblies of God or a single Latin America missions agency.
3. It does not mean that as Assemblies of God we give up our identity and working philosophy to satisfy other missionary movements.
4. It does not mean that because of pressure of the ecclesiastical community, raising up local and national churches in the mission field that are without a direct identity and affiliation with other Assemblies of God local and national churches.

What cooperation DOES mean to us:

1. It does mean communication between us, and sharing our support and respect to other missionary movements in the body of Christ, even when they have a different philosophy of work.
2. It does mean respecting the national church of the Assemblies of God that already exists, and not raising up diverse and various national churches of the Assemblies of God in a single country and/or people group. (For example, a Brazilian Assemblies of God, a Korean Assemblies of God, a Nigerian Assemblies of God, etc.)
3. It does mean uniting the missionary efforts of the Assemblies of God of different countries with the purpose of establishing, developing, and serving one National Assemblies of God Church in the field, and yet giving freedom to the development of different missionary

ministries, as the diversity of God's gifts are given for the edification of the national work.
4. It does mean communicating between missions departments and agencies of Latin America and the world, respecting the autonomy of every nation.

THEREFORE, considering that the Assemblies of God has doctrine and philosophy in common, and that the challenges of the world are great, we must recognize the urgency of cooperation between the missions departments/agencies of the Assemblies of God of our countries, taking advantage of the resources, contacts, and experiences of all of us combined.

AS WELL, considering that there are many unreached people groups that lack a national church; however, at the same time, there are many national churches already established in many mission fields that must be respected by those that come from other countries, we must concern ourselves with establishing the national church together with other missionary efforts of the Assemblies of God already established in the receiving country, and when a national church already exists, all of our missionary effort should be to strengthen and support it.

## Appendix 4
## Missions Together:
## An Intensive Training Seminar for Missional Leaders
(Translated from Spanish: "Misiones En Conjunto")

**Theme:** Missionary Leadership for the 21st Century: From Negligence to Diligence: Being an Effective Missions Leader

**Purpose:** To provide basic missions training to leadership

Those who should attend:
1. Members of the missions department
2. Missions promoters
3. National church executives
4. Bible School directors and any teachers involved with missions training in the Bible Schools
5. Interested potential leaders

**Total teaching:** 20-30 hours, according to the country's situation and proposal

**Teachers:** Members of the MEC Latin America Missions Commission

### Basic Contents of Seminar and Training:

1. Profile of a missions leader
2. Organization and advances of missions in the Assemblies of God of Latin America and as well the worldwide Assemblies of God
3. Affirmation of the basic theological foundation for missions
4. Organizational chart of different missions departments in Latin America and the responsibilities of each of the members
5. The importance of having a basic philosophy and guidelines for your missions department and documenting it in a missions manual
6. The basic task of organizing an office that will serve the churches and the missionaries

7. Forming support programs for your missions department (future missionaries, national promoters, intercessors, "children's missions vision," etc.)
8. Strategies of missions mobilization (promotion and forming an army of promoters)
9. Generating finances for missions and teaching on the faith promise
10. Resources of missionary formation
11. Uses of technology in doing and promoting missions
12. Challenges in the task of world evangelization
13. Pastoral care and overall care for the missionaries, by the local church and missions department
14. Goals, plans, and projects, for the short and long term
15. How to evaluate your missions department: Where you are at today, needed changes that are urgent, and what are your plans for the short and long term?
** Other subjects can be considered at the request of the missions department receiving the teaching

# Appendix 5
# Missionary Categories

## MISSIONARY CATEGORIES – A Latin Country – 2010

| CATEGORY TYPE | ECONOMIC RELATIONSHIP | AMOUNT OF TIME ON FIELD | TIME OF DEPUTATION WHEN HOME | REQUIREMENTS FOR SCHOOL OF MISSIONS | OBSERVATIONS |
|---|---|---|---|---|---|
| FULLY APPOINTED | Fully supported from sending country | 3 years, 4 years possible upon request | 6-12 months | Required during deputation | |
| MISSIONARY IN TRAINING | Fully supported from sending country | 3 years first term | 6-12 months | Required during deputation | First term: under supervision of a mentor. After: promoted to fully appointed |
| SHORT TERM | Fully supported from sending country | 1 year, renewable for a 2$^{nd}$ year | 6 months | Required before leaving | Must be under the supervision of a missionary |
| MISSIONARY PASTOR | Support can be shared by the local church they pastor | 5 years and then renewable | Flexible according to need and situation | Required at least once every 5 years | Must be submissive to DNM and not just to receiving country |
| MINISTERIAL SUPPORT | Support can be shared by the local church they pastor | 5 years and then renewable | Flexible according to need and situation | Required at least once every 5 years | Must be in full time ministry without secular employment |
| BI-VOCATIONAL | Receives most of their support from work | 5 years and then renewable | Flexible according to work and situation | Required at least once every 5 years | Though they do not depend on sending country, they can receive offerings |
| ETHNIC GROUPS IN COUNTRY | Can receive support from churches | Ongoing as need requires | Flexible according to the situation | Required at least once every 5 years | Is within the country but to another culture/ethnic group |

## Appendix 6
## Compassion and Justice in the Old Testament
## William Kirsch

In the Old Testament compassion and justice generally seem to be related to one's response to God and occasionally to what one does not do. Exodus 33:19 addresses the sovereignty of God when it says, "I will have mercy upon whom I have mercy and compassion on whom I have compassion." This passage is repeated in Romans 9:14-15, where it seems to indicate a spiritual, not physical, compassion through salvation. Although this may appear arbitrary, we know from the full counsel of Scripture that God responds to individuals based upon their response to Him. Deuteronomy 13:17 indicates compassion is first and foremost addressed to humankind's greatest need, their sinful condition, as it should be. This same sentiment is also expressed in other passages (Deut. 30:3; 32:36; Judg. 2:18; 2 Kings 13:23; 2 Chron. 30:9; Neh. 9:19, 27-28; Psa. 51:1; 77:9; 102:13; 103:4; Isa. 4:1; Jonah 3:9-10; 4:1).

Some further Old Testament examples include the following:

- Asking for compassion for sins, as opposed to physical relief (Psa. 90:13)
- Both spiritual and physical compassion (Psa. 116:5; 119:77, 156)
- Physical situation based on obedience (Psa. 135:14)
- The general compassionate nature of God to all people (Psa. 145:9; Lam. 3:32)
- God's desire to show compassion on those who are just (Isa. 30:18)
- Israel is shown compassion when they are obedient (Isa. 49:10-15; 51:3; 54:7-8, 10; 60:10; 63:7, 15; Jer. 12:15; 30:18; 31:20; 33:26; 42:12; Ezek. 39:25; Hos. 2:19; 11:8; 14:3, Mic. 7:19).
- God has no compassion for evil (i.e., for Babylon: Isa. 13:18, Jer. 21:7).
- God has no compassion for Israel in rebellion (Isa. 27:11; Jer. 13:14; 15:6; Ezek. 9:5; 16:5; Hos. 13:14; Amos 1:11 [for idolaters]).
- We are to show compassion by not oppressing others (Zach. 7:9-10).

Typically justice is shown in injunctions against perverting it by not taking advantage of another as opposed to helping someone in need. This applies especially to the poor, oppressed, fatherless, widows, and aliens. Thus justice is typically invoked as an injunction against taking advantage of others rather than a command to help them out of an unjust situation. However, although less often referenced but equally important, is the proactive element of defending the cause of those who experience injustice (Isa. 1:16-17).

## Appendix 7
## [Cover Letter for Resolution Calling for an AAGA World Missions Commission]

December 1, 1999

Rev. Charles Osueke
Chairman, Africa Assemblies of God Alliance
P.O. Box 395
Enugu, Enugu State
Nigeria, West Africa

Dear Rev. Osueke and members of the AAGA Executive:

Greetings in the strong name of Jesus!

We are sure that you brethren, along with each of us and many others, sense the evident leading of the Holy Spirit upon the churches of Africa to take an aggressive role in the fulfillment of the Great Commission. It is truly a pivotal moment for the Church in Africa. In God's divine plan He is calling loudly for the churches of Africa to take their place in history's long march of missionary endeavor, more than we have ever before.

In order to facilitate the current moving of God's Spirit, which is so evident, we, the undersigned respectfully submit the enclosed resolution for the prayerful and thoughtful consideration of the AAGA Executive, hopefully in your upcoming meeting in Lomé, Togo in January 2000. The resolution calls for the creation of an AAGA World Missions Commission. In our resolution, the AAGA WMC would serve to facilitate and coordinate Assemblies of God missions efforts across the continent.

You will discover that our proposal is very simple. Our prayer is that its simplicity will allow for the earliest possible implementation of developmental efforts to establish AAGA WMC. It is our hope that provisional approval can be given by the AAGA Executive, pending full approval of the AAGA General Assembly in Indianapolis in August 2000.

Respectfully submitted,

| | | |
|---|---|---|
| Donald Tucker | John York | John Ikoni |
| AAGA Exe. Secretary | ATTS Director Nigeria | Gen. Secretary |
| Resolution Sponsor | Resolution Sponsor | Resolution Sponsor |

## Appendix 8
## RESOLUTION
### [Calling for the Establishment of the World Missions Commission]

Missionary work has been undertaken by the churches of Africa for decades. There is presently, however, great advancement in widespread recognition of the Great Commission as the mandate for the world-wide Church, including Africa. Several national churches among the Assemblies of God have developed specific missions programs and moved intentionally into implementing plans of action. In as much as the AAGA Charter contains a stated intention to serve in a vital capacity in the planning and implementation of international missionary endeavors from and within the African continent, as well as to nations beyond Africa as God leads,

BE IT THEREFORE RESOLVED that the AAGA WORLD MISSIONS COMMISSION, hereinafter referred to simply as AAGA/MC, be established with the following purposes in view…

1) Prioritizing efforts to reach unreached peoples by the national churches of Africa, addressing the following specific areas of need.
    a) Research into the location and nature of all of Africa's unreached peoples, wherever they may be found.
    b) Sourcing accurate and useful statistics and information on unreached peoples to the national church missions agencies across Africa.
    c) Allocating primary missions responsibility for specific unreached peoples to those national churches interested and ready by August 2000.
    d) Charting the progress in reaching Africa's unreached peoples.
    e) Developing appropriate printed materials to support the mandated missions efforts.

2) Provide coordination of existing and new missionary endeavors across the continent through the following activities, as a service to the national churches of Africa.

a) Maintain a data base of current missionary endeavors being actively pursued across the continent as well as those missionary endeavors projected for future implementation.
b) Provide an official listing of all Assemblies of God missionaries representing Assemblies of God national churches, including their place of assignment, ministry activity, and length of service.
c) Serve as a forum for discussion, strategic planning, decision-making and conflict resolution concerning the deployment of national church missionary personnel across the continent.

3) Encourage the establishment and function of regional missions departments, along the geographical divisions of the official AAGA regions (a total of five at this time) with the following intentions.
a) The ongoing implementation of the "Eleventh Hour Institute" concept of mission training in each region of the continent, and in individual countries requesting the same, in close collaboration with ATTS as the leading agency in this function. A timetable for implementation of the EHI program should be established as a first priority of the AAGA/MC.
b) The development of an AAGA Research effort, focused upon world missions efforts, but not limited to that function.

SPECIFIC PROPOSALS

1) Five commission members should be selected and appointed by the AAGA Executive to accomplish the functions listed above.
2) Commission members will serve under the direction of the AAGA Executive and at their disposition entirely, including the establishment of term length.
3) Electronic mail should be utilized as a source of ongoing contact to keep travel for meetings, and the resulting expenditures, at a minimum.
4) Two at-large commission members should be added to the five appointed delegates, one coming from the AAGA Executive and the other a representative of ATTS.
5) Commission members should be selected and empowered to function during the January 2000 AAGA Executive meeting with ratification to be sought in August 2000 in the General Assembly in Indianapolis.

# Appendix 9
# Africa Assemblies of God Alliance
# World Missions Commission

## CONSTITUTION

The Africa Assemblies of God Alliance (AAGA) Charter contains a stated intention to serve in a vital capacity in the planning and implementation of international missionary endeavors within the continent of Africa as well as to nations beyond Africa as well. In fulfillment of that stated intention the AAGA World Missions Commission has been formed.

ARTICLE I: Name

The name shall be AAGA World Missions Commission, conveniently referred to as the AAGA WMC.

ARTICLE II: Mandate
- A. The clear mandate of the AAGA WMC, expressed by the official documents of AAGA, is to facilitate and encourage the missionary enterprises of our national churches across Africa by every means possible. These shall include, but shall not be limited to, information development, promotional efforts and coordination on the continental, regional, and/or national level. A priority objective in the commission's mandate shall be to create and maintain a continent-wide training effort in missiology at every level of the church, patterned after the principles employed in the current Eleventh Hour Institute concept.
- B. A Focus on Mandate document shall be prepared as an addendum to this constitution to serve as the official procedural outline for the fulfillment of the AAGA WMC mandate and to assure a sharp focus on the commission's purpose.

ARTICLE III: Composition
- A. The AAGA WMC shall be composed of
  - One representative from each of the current administrative, geographical, or linguistic regions currently viable in the structure of AAGA.

- One at large representative from the AAGA Executive Committee.
- One at large representative from the Africa Theological Training Services (ATTS)
  B. Membership
    - Regional representatives of the AAGA WMC shall be appointed by the regional AAGA structure and ratified by the AAGA Executive Committee.
    - At large representatives shall be appointed by the appropriated entity which they represent and ratified by the AAGA Executive Committee.

ARTICLE IV: Terms of Service
  A. Appointments to the AAGA WMC shall be for four years, renewable without limitation.
  B. Vacancies shall be filled by interim appointment by the AAGA Executive Committee until such time as the regional AAGA organization where the vacancy has occurred can appoint a replacement.
  C. A membership position on the commission may be declared vacant due to the resignation or removal of a member. The AAGA Executive Committee due to inactivity, dereliction of commission responsibilities, or other valid reasons officially minuted by the AAGA Executive Committee may remove a member.

ARTICLE V: Meetings
  A. Meetings shall be convened as necessary, but no less than once yearly. In order to maintain the lowest level of expenses, the electronic media (fax transmissions, email, etc.) should be used to conduct the activities of AAGA WMC as much as possible.
  B. A quorum for matters requiring a vote or consensus agreement of the commission will require 2/3 of the commission members. A quorum can be verified by either physical presence or electronic communications when electronic media is employed.
  C. A recording secretary, selected from among and by the commission appointees, shall maintain written records of the deliberations, decisions, and implementations of the AAGA WMC.

D. Travel and other expenses related to the work of individual commission members is the responsibility of the region or entity represented.
E. Quarterly, written summaries of commission activities shall be submitted to the AAGA Executive Committee. When the AAGA WMC meets in formal session, official minutes shall be kept and forwarded to the AAGA Executive Committee and concerned parties as deemed necessary by the AAGA WMC or as instructed by the AAGA WMC.

ARTICLE VI: Leadership
A. A chairman shall be selected by the commission members to facilitate meetings and communications for the work of the commission.
B. A recording secretary shall be selected by the commission members to maintain and circulate the mandated quarterly summaries and official minutes, as well as all necessary written correspondence as he/she may be assigned.
C. A treasurer may be selected in reference to Article VII, Paragraph C.

ARTICLE VII: Finances
A. The mandate of the AAGA WMC, as stated in the official documents of AAGA, shall focus on information development, promotional efforts, and coordination. Fund raising for the purpose of financing missionary efforts may be an activity assumed by the commission in due time. Direct fund raising by the commission for the purpose of financing missionary efforts is not within the initial mandate. However, counsel and assistance with fund raising by national churches is a valid service which the commission may offer.
B. The financial resources required for the commission's activities shall be provided by donations from member churches, partner entities interested in the development of the missionary outreach of our national churches, or from the AAGA treasury as resources permit.
C. In order to permit the AAGA WMC to focus on their stated mandate as unencumbered as possible, the AAGA Executive Committee Treasurer shall administer the financial concerns of the commission initially. At such time as deemed appropriate, a treasurer can be appointed from among the commission membership.

D. Regular financial reporting concerning AAGA WMC shall be included in the financial reporting of the AAGA Executive Committee until such time a decision is made to establish a separate reporting procedure for AAGA WMC finances.

ARTICLE VIII: Amendments
  A. Amendments to the constitution can be offered by commission members, members of the AAGA Executive Committee, or any voting member of AAGA.
  B. Amendments require a 2/3 vote of the AAGA voting membership in any duly called assembly.

ARTICLE IX: Cessation of Activities
  A. Activities of the AAGA WMC will cease upon a formal decision by the AAGA Executive Committee until ratification of such decision can be made by the AAGA membership in session.
  B. Should activities of the AAGA WMC cease, all material and financial resources of the AAGA WMC shall remain in the possession of AAGA.

# Appendix 10
# Pentecostal World Missions Consultation
# List of Participants

Zebulon Alulu, Kenya
Uche Ama, Nigeria
Greg Beggs, Kenya
Dick Brogden, Sudan
Gaylord Brown, Malawi
Lazarus Chakwera, Malawi
Lawrence Chipao, Malawi
Edward Chitsonga, Malawi
Michael Dissanayeke, Sri Lanka
Scott Hanson, Tanzania
Ken Krucker, USA
Bill Kirsch, USA
Bill Kuert, Kenya
Doug Lowenberg, Kenya
Enson Lwesya, Malawi
Jackson Mbuthia, Kenya
Bob McCully, Sudan
Denzil R. Miller, USA
Bill Moore, USA
Jeff Nelson, Kenya
Peter Njiri, Kenya
Peter Nuthu, Kenya
Antonio Pedrozo, Argentina
Weston Sambo, Tanzania
Randy Tarr, Senegal
Pius Tembu, Kenya
Jim Thacker, USA

# Contributors

**Uchechukwu Ama**

Uchechukwu (Uche) Ama is Director of Evangelism and Missions for the Central Africa Assemblies of God Alliance. He previously served as Secretary for the Assemblies of God Nigeria Decade of Harvest emphasis (1990-2000). He also served as the National Coordinator for Research and Information (1992-2002) and as the National Director of Corporate Planning and Ministries for the Assemblies of God Nigeria (2002-2010). He is a team member of the Acts in Africa Initiative.

**Richard Brogden**

Dick Brogden is team leader for the Assemblies of God World Missions church-planting teams in East Africa. For the past 19 years he has worked among Muslims in Africa. He and his family were founding leaders of the Khartoum Christian Center, and other missionary ministries in East Africa Brogden has published four books, contributed chapters to various anthologies, and written for the *International Journal of Frontier Mission*.

**Lazarus M. Chakwera**

Dr. Lazarus Chakwera is President of the Malawi Assemblies of God. He has distinguished himself as a passionate and practical missiologist in Africa and beyond. He led in development of the Eleventh Hour Institute and worked as its founding president. He serves on various missions and educational boards including the World Assemblies of God Fellowship (secretary), the Africa Assemblies of God Alliance (chairman), the Association for Pentecostal Theological Education in Africa (chairman), and Pan-Africa Theological Seminary (chairman). He is founding senior pastor of International Christian Assembly in Lilongwe, Malawi. His books include, *Reach the Nations*, *Islam and Animism,* and *Advanced Studies in the Biblical Theology of Missions*.

**William Kirsch**

Dr. William (Bill) Kirsch is a team leader for Africa's Hope, a ministry assisting more than 200 residential and extension schools across Africa. He has served as academic dean at Cape Theological Seminary in Cape Town, South Africa, and as teacher and administrator at Assembly Bible College in Gaborone, Botswana. Bill serves as the AGWM team leader for Gabon and travels extensively throughout Africa consulting with schools, teaching, and conducting leadership training seminars. He is author of the book, *Pentateuch*.

## Douglas Lowenburg

Dr. Douglas Lowenburg is the director and dean of the East Africa Graduate Studies Centre in Nairobi, Kenya, and a non-resident faculty member of Pan-Africa Theological Seminary. He taught cross-cultural ministries at North Central University in Minneapolis. He and his wife, Corrine, have served as a missionaries to Burkina Faso and Ethiopia, where he was principal of Addis Ababa Bible College. During their time in Africa they have worked in Bible college and seminary training. They have also done pastoral ministry in Ethiopia, Togo, and Kenya.

## Andrew Mkwaila

Andrew Mkwaila is a credentialed minister with the Malawi Assemblies of God. He is currently serving as Pastor of Mission at Cornerstone Church (Assemblies of God) in Okemos, Michigan. He also works with Help for the Harvest, an ministry aimed at fostering increased missional awareness in local churches. Previously he planted and pastored a church in Lilongwe, Malawi. He has a M.A. in Intercultural Studies (2009) from All Nations Theological Seminary and is pursuing a doctorate in missiology at Fuller Theological Seminary.

## Enson Mbilikile Lwesya

Dr. Enson Lwesya is director of the Africa Assemblies of God Alliance, World Missions Commission. He also serves as director of the All Nations Theological Seminary in Lilongwe, Malawi, and as executive minister at the International Christian Assembly in the same city. From 2001-2007 Lwesya served as principal and instructor at the Assemblies of God School of Theology in Lilongwe. He travels extensively in Africa teaching in Eleventh Hour Institutes and Acts in Africa conferences. Lwesya has authored four books, including, *Dreaming Your Future, Flames of Fire, Leading Christian Organi-*

*zations,* and *Why Africans Fail to Lead.*

## Denzil R. Miller

Dr. Denzil (Denny) R. Miller is director of the Acts in Africa Initiative, a ministry commissioned by the Africa Assemblies of God Alliance to coordinate the Africa Assemblies of God "Decade of Pentecost" emphasis (2010-2020). He travels extensively throughout Africa teaching and preaching in missions and leadership conferences. He has authored several books and developed and taught seminary courses on the work of the Holy Spirit in the life of the believer and in the work of missions. His books include *Power Encounter, In Step with the Spirit, Empowered for Global Mission, The Kingdom and the Power, The Spirit of God in Mission: A Vocational Commentary on the Book of Acts,* and *Teaching in the Spirit.*

## Antonio Pedrozo

Antonio (Tony) Pedrozo is an executive member of the Argentine Assemblies of God Missions Department and Area Supervisor for Africa and Asia. After their appointment by the Argentine Assemblies of God in 1994, he and his wife, Millie, served as missionaries in Zaire and Chad. Their work included working with Rwandese refugees, church planting, and pastoral training. While in Chad Pedrozo started the country's first Christian FM Radio station named the Voice of Hope. He has also used his skills as a nurse practitioner in his missionary work.

## Brad Walz

Brad Walz is president of the Argentine Assemblies of God Missions Department, which has become the largest missions sending agency in Latin America with more than 150 workers sent to 35 nations. In 2009 the department became the first missions agency in Latin America to surpass a million dollars in offerings in one calendar year. Walz is also president of the AG Latin Missions Network, "Misiones en Conjunto" (Missions Together), and chairman of the World Assemblies of God Fellowship Missions Commission.

**Other Decade of Pentecost Publications
Available from AIA Publications:**

*Proclaiming Pentecost: 100 Sermon Outlines
on the Power of Pentecost*

*Experiencing the Spirit: A Study of the Work of the Holy
Spirit in the Life of the Believer*

*You Can Minister in God's Power: A Guide
for Spirit-filled Disciples*

*Power for Mission: The Africa Assemblies of God
Mobilizing to Reach the Unreached*

*L'universalisation des missions pentecôtistes
en Afrique : Le mouvement missionnaire émergent
au sein des Assemblées de Dieu d'Afrique*

for further information visit
www.DecadeofPentecost.org

AIA Publications
580D Central Street
Springfield, MO 65802

www.ingramcontent.com/pod-product-compliance
Lightning Source LLC
Chambersburg PA
CBHW061643040426
42446CB00010B/1561